Life is a Game of Inches

CHRISTIAN ROBERTS WITH JAMES LEIGHTON

VERTICAL EDITIONS

www.verticaleditions.com

DEDICATION

In beloved memory of Richard John Roberts, 'Pops',
1946–2008.

First published in the United Kingdom in 2010 by
Vertical Editions, Unit 4a, Snaygill Industrial
Estate, Skipton, North Yorkshire BD23 2QR

www.verticaleditions.com

ISBN 978-1-904091-44-8

A CIP catalogue record for this book is available
from the British Library

Cover design and typeset by HBA, York

Printed and bound by JF Print Limited, Somerset

CONTENTS

Prologue 9

1. Early Days 15

2. Getting into Football 32

3. Best Days of my Life 48

4. Highs and Lows 57

5. Going Downhill 70

6. A Fresh Start 81

7. Moving up in the World 97

8. Alcohol Takes a Grip 104

9. Reporting for Duty 120

10. The Descent 125

11. Moving On 137

12. The Abyss 148

13. Giving Life a Chance 155

14. Rediscovering the Game that I Loved 176

15. Things Take a Turn for the Worse 197

16. A Year to Forget 210

17. Looking to the Future 223

Appendix: Career Statistics 232

ACKNOWLEDGEMENTS

There are literally too many people to thank who have been a huge part of my life in and out of football. I hope everyone who has helped me on my way knows how much I appreciate them. Below are just a few names of people who have really gone beyond the call of duty and I thank them with all my heart.

Mr Richards 'Rocko'
My school PE teacher who encouraged and inspired me.

Gavin Tait and Gwynn Williams
My youth coaches at Cardiff City who spotted me and gave me a chance.

Noel Blake and John Cornforth
For giving me the opportunity to resurrect my career at Exeter City.

Danny Wilson
For being one of the nicest guys in football and for putting up with me when I probably didn't deserve it.

Iffy Onoura
For rescuing me from alcoholism and providing me with invaluable support after treatment.

Sporting Chance Clinic

Without the help of the staff at the Sporting Chance Clinic I dread to think where I would be now.

Dennis Wise and Gus Poyet

For believing in me when others would have cast me aside.

Richard Shepherd, Cardiff City and Chris Tanner, Swindon Town

For their help with a number of photographs.

James Leighton

For putting my story into words.

Vertical Editions

For believing in my story and being a pleasure to work with.

Last and by no means least, thank you to the fans of Cardiff City, Exeter City, Bristol City and Swindon Town. You were all unbelievable to me!

PROLOGUE

As each person stood up to introduce themselves I really didn't know what I was going to say. To be honest, not only was I desperately nervous at being sat in a room full of strangers, but also my ego and bravado had withered away. Usually I had an answer for everything. In here I was blank. I kept thinking to myself, 'What am I doing with these pissheads? I don't belong here!'

It was only my second day in treatment at the Sporting Chance Clinic and I was sent here, to an Alcoholics Anonymous (AA) meeting. I didn't really understand what I was doing at the meeting as all these people were hardcore drinkers and I wasn't in the same class as them. These guys could never touch a drink again in their lives whilst I was hoping simply to cut back on my drinking.

Most of them were telling desperate stories about their alcohol addiction and how they had lost everything. On the other hand, I had recently played for Bristol City at the Millennium Stadium; I had a big house, a beautiful wife, two wonderful kids and was earning good money. What could possibly be so wrong with my life that I needed to seek help amongst these losers?

Some people thought that I had a problem with alcohol. Yes, I liked a drink, and at times it had caused me to do some stupid things, but you could say the same for most people. Who hasn't had a drink and done something that they regret? Anyway, I didn't necessarily think that I had a serious problem with alcohol. If I could just learn to limit my drinking to a couple of pints a day then everything would be fine.

Fair enough, I had been drinking a bit too much lately but it had been a rough couple of months. I had separated from my wife and my old club Bristol City had let me go. My confidence was understandably at a low ebb so I sought solace in having a few drinks. Admittedly I had overstepped the mark a bit, and I recognised that, so I checked myself into rehab.

When I arrived at the clinic I underwent a medical. Usually my weight was in the region of 12 stone 8 pounds and my body fat was around 12%. Finding out that I was two stone overweight, and that my body fat percentage was twice what it should be was a bit surprising. I was meant to be a professional footballer so I was disappointed that I had let myself go. It wasn't a problem though, I may have been overweight but they couldn't say that was solely due to my alcohol consumption. My attitude in training recently had been poor, and my diet had been atrocious, so that would explain my gain in weight. When I left the clinic I was confident that I could shed the pounds and everything would be back to normal.

During the medical I told the doctor that I had recently undergone a liver test at my club, Swindon Town, and that my liver score was 66. I later found out that the score in a healthy person was meant to be 26, which was unnerving, but it wasn't anything that couldn't be sorted.

Something that had been worrying me for a while was the fact that I kept vomiting and urinating blood. I told the doctor about it, and he looked concerned, but I was sure that if I took a tablet or something then these things would sort themselves out. I convinced myself that it was probably an infection of some sort and I was confident that it had nothing to do with my alcohol consumption.

The doctor asked me how many units of alcohol I was drinking each week. Every week day I was probably drinking an average of around 15 pints of Stella and then on weekends it could be up to 25 pints a day. A rough estimate was that I was therefore getting through over 350 units of alcohol each week. When he told me that the maximum units of alcohol an adult male should consume in a week was 28, the equivalent of 9.5 pints of Stella, I was shocked.

Before attending the AA meeting I had undergone therapy with one of the clinic's therapists, Julian Keeling. During the sessions we discussed events in my life that had occurred because of drinking.

One of the first things that we talked about was when I had taken my seven-year-old son, Ethan, to a kids' play group in a local leisure centre. Whilst I was sat down, merry after a few beers, I heard a loud scream and it turned out to be my son. When I saw him I was a bit worried because his leg was at an angle and he was in absolute agony. With him shaking and screaming I carried him in my arms to my car, drove him home and put him on the sofa where he continued to cry.

My wife, Janine, told me that I needed to take him to the hospital as he had clearly broken his leg. I was adamant that it was just a bruise, even though I knew it was worse than that, and I told her that he would get

11

over it. Yet Ethan wouldn't calm down, he was red in the face and kept screaming and crying. In the end Janine told me in no uncertain terms that I had to take him to a doctor. I was meant to be going to the pub, and had been looking forward to having a few Stellas, so I blew my top.

After a blazing row I told Janine that I would drop her off down the hospital with Ethan and that I would then look after our three-year-old son, Ewan. After taking them to the hospital I still fancied a drink so I dropped Ewan off at my father's and went to the pub. As I was getting stuck into my fifth pint I heard that Ethan had snapped his tibia and fibula in his leg. That upset me so I decided that I needed a few more drinks to deal with the bad news. I didn't go home that night.

I then told Julian about when I had been on a 48-hour session and was waiting for the doors to open at my local pub on the Sunday morning. My wife and I had separated at the time, and it was my day to see the kids, so she dropped them off at the pub so that they could spend the day with me.

After days of non-stop binging I was absolutely hammered, and still had a good few hours drinking left in me, so seeing the kids was a bit of an inconvenience. I thought I could keep them quiet by buying them some food at the pub and then that way I could continue to drink. When Janine arrived, and saw the state of me, she kicked off and took the kids away. 'Why's she trying to show me up in front of my mates?' I thought with all the cloudy brained logic of a man who was seeing the world through beer soaked spectacles. No one shows me up in front of my mates and walks away, so in order to save my pride I tried to humiliate her. Without thinking I launched my pint glass at her, but it missed, and struck another woman. I didn't care; I turned my back and walked away. I was indestructible.

Julian asked whether my drinking had ever affected my career. I admitted that I had missed a few days training because of hangovers but then who hasn't missed work at some point because they were worse for wear through drink? As we discussed it further I started to realise that for most of the last two years I had trained and played when I was drunk.

One game in particular came to mind, a cup clash with Watford, when I was playing for Bristol City. The game was on a Tuesday night and I had been out drinking since Saturday evening. The first time that I actually got some sleep, since I had gone out, was when I staggered home at 11.00am on Tuesday morning. Even after a few hours' sleep I was still shit faced but that didn't stop me driving to Ashton Gate, from my home in Cardiff, and putting in the worst display of my career. Booze was seeping out of my pores, I was sweating pure Stella and I was still so drunk that I was running in all sorts of directions. The only thing that got me through the game was knowing that a nice cold pint would be waiting for me in the players' bar afterwards.

'When was the last time I had actually been totally sober at training?' I thought to myself. It had certainly been a good few years and training in that condition meant that I was usually low on energy so as a result I wouldn't make much effort. If the manager had a pop at me I would go berserk, I didn't see a problem with how I was performing. In time this meant that I would be dropped from the team and would lead to Bristol City selling me to Swindon Town. It wasn't my problem though; the manager was picking on me.

Julian then asked if my drinking had ever affected my marriage. At the time I had been separated from my wife for around four months. When he asked me the reason for the separation I initially couldn't honestly tell him. Then it came to me, I was so fed up with hiding how much I was drinking I thought it would be easier if I left my wife and kids so I could drink as much as I wanted. That certainly did the trick, as I no longer had to hide bottles of wine in cupboards, I could drink until I collapsed with no one shouting at me.

We then discussed the subject of my finances. I had been earning good money at both Swindon and Bristol over the last four years so why was I broke? The only answer that I could give him was that I had spent all my money on alcohol. I had blown all my savings and wages, maxed numerous credit cards, taken out loans I couldn't afford to pay back and owed money to all sorts of people all over the place. My finances were so dire that one month I even told Janine that I hadn't been paid as I couldn't tell her that I had blown my month's wages on booze.

As I sat in that AA meeting, reflecting on everything that I had discussed in therapy, it suddenly dawned on me, I had a problem. I had lost my family, my money, my health and my career to alcohol.

When it finally came to my turn to speak I stood up, took a deep breath and for the first time said the words, 'My name is Christian Roberts and I'm an alcoholic'.

1

EARLY DAYS

My story begins way back in 1977, before I was even a twinkle in my dad's eye, when Margaret Thatcher just won her first election and Liverpool were sweeping all before them at home and in Europe. My old man had turned 30, around the age I am now, and he was in the process of getting divorced from his first wife with whom he had two children, my step-brothers, Daryl and David.

As well as getting divorced my Dad also suffered a nasty accident at the steelworks, where he worked, which resulted in him losing his big toe. In a weird way it was a blessing in disguise because with the compensation money he received he was able to buy my grandfather's house in a council estate called Llanrumney in Cardiff. Without that money it was extremely unlikely that my Dad would have ever been able to afford a house, certainly nothing as nice as the one that he bought.

With his career at the steelworks at an end, my Dad became a handyman on building sites, basically doing bits and bobs here and there to earn whatever money he could. He wasn't particularly gifted with any talents; but he was a grafter and worked hard to get a wage. The unique gift he had, and in my opinion it's the best gift that a human being can have, was the man that he was. Dad was a man of values and principles and never cheated anyone. He certainly set a great example to me.

Not long after getting divorced he met my mother, Damiana, who was only 19 years old at the time. Despite the 11-year age difference they soon began a relationship that saw them get married. My father was a skinny, quiet man whilst my Mother was a beautiful and bubbly girl from a mixed parentage background who had all the boys after her. It's true when they say that opposites attract because on paper their relationship should never have worked but somehow it did.

After getting married, Mum and Dad moved into the house in Llanrumney and had their first child, Matthew. Within a year I was born and my parents had another mouth to feed. My Dad was a traditional man and wanted Mum to stay at home to raise the two of us so it was down to him to provide for the family.

I think at this stage he was probably earning around £140.00 a week but he told Mum that he only earned £110.00. He always told me, 'Wives don't have to know everything', and looking back at my own experiences he was probably right.

He wouldn't squander the £30 he saved on himself; he hid it under the carpet in his bedroom and used it as an emergency fund. That way, if he hadn't earned as much as he had expected, he always had some money to fall back on which would allow us to eat. Some weeks my old man could sell some scrap steel or lead he had picked up on a job and that extra cash would make us feel like millionaires as we could afford to buy a few treats that were normally out of our reach.

Mum also did a bit of work on the side to help out the family. She was good at organising things and I remember she did a few catering jobs for the Chartered Trust and helped organise parties and events. She was also the person in the community people visited if they needed help filling in forms. I didn't know what they were at the time but looking back they were probably benefit forms.

Everyone in the community seemed to have a different talent back then and they would all be there for each other. My Mum was the person to go to for forms whilst other people on the estate would help with other things. It was a close-knit community and everyone knew one another. Llanrumney was a great place to grow up, it was tough and tight at times but it made me the person I am today. It certainly made me realise the value of everyone looking out for each other. With everyone mucking in we hardly ever went without the necessities.

If people knew you were hard up, but from a good family, they turned a blind eye to certain things. For instance, my mates and me used to like going to the swimming pool in the local leisure centre but my Mum couldn't always afford to give me the £1.00 entry fee. If that was the case I would sneak under the barrier as quickly as I could so that the lady in reception couldn't see me. I thought I was some kind of arch criminal continually getting away with it but little did I know. A few years ago I saw the lady from the reception area and she told me, 'I used to watch you sneak under the barrier but I let you in as I knew you couldn't afford it'.

My Mum and Dad were both popular and seemed

to be well liked in the neighbourhood. Our house was a social gathering point and I swear we must have had everyone from Llanrumney in our living room at some point. The door was always open and my Dad would sometimes bring back people from the pub, who he had only just met, and my Mum would cook them all some food. It was mad, but I loved it, and I suppose it made me the sociable, outgoing person that I am today as I'm always comfortable with strangers, in part due to my upbringing.

As a nipper I was always closer to my Mum rather than my Dad. Dad terrified me as he ran a tight ship and wouldn't stand for any messing around. My Mum, on the other hand, was a lot more laid back, probably, in part, due to her liking a drink.

At the time I didn't really think anything of my Mum's drinking habits, in fact I thought all adults drank like she did. However, looking back now it's obvious that she had some sort of drink problem. Some days I would wake up for school, and I would need her to iron a shirt for me, but she would still be hungover from drinking the day before and wouldn't be in a fit state to do anything until she had a drink of cider. This was at 8.00am!

When we didn't have any cider in the house I had to bomb down to the local shop on my BMX, where the owners knew me, and they would give me a bottle of cider to take back home for my Mum. Only after she had her drink would she be able to iron me a shirt for school.

Alcohol was a constant presence in our lives. My grandfather, Nathaniel, always sat in our back room with a small glass of rum and went through a bottle of the stuff every day whilst my Dad also enjoyed a drink and spent a lot of time in the pub with his mates. That's just the way it was and I didn't think anything of it.

Although my Mum never seemed to be without a drink in her hand she was a hard working, genuine woman who would cut her arm off for you. If I asked for 50p to go up the shops to get some sweets she would give it to me even if it was the last 50p that she had. If we were sick she would look after us and I can honestly say that she cared for us and we felt loved. But despite this, some nights, she would be so wasted she wouldn't be able to cook any food for us. On Monday, Wednesday and Friday my Dad was usually down the pub, catching up with his mates, so if Mum was unable to cook Matthew and me had to fend for ourselves.

On those nights we would go down to the local shop, which was run by two cracking guys called Keith and Derrick, and they would look after us. They loved my Mum, but I think they were aware of her drink issues, so if we went in the shop they would give us a pasty, some crisps, a chocolate bar and a can of coke. I don't like to think about how we would have got by some nights if it weren't for them. It's fair to say they were a vital part of our lives and I don't think they can ever truly appreciate how grateful I am to them.

For some reason I always had different opinions on Mum and Dad's drinking habits. In my eyes my Dad was a working man and I believe that any man is entitled to a cold beer after a day's work. After all, that's what the tradition in this country has always been for the working class. Most importantly though, I didn't see my Dad as having a drink problem; he could stop drinking whenever he wanted. On a number of occasions he would happily drink a pint of squash when he was in the pub and even if he did have a drink he rarely went over the top. Alcohol never seemed to affect my Dad's life, he went to work every single day and he would never put alcohol before his family.

My Mum's drinking on the other hand affected almost everything that she did. She constantly had to have a drink nearby and she couldn't function unless there was alcohol inside her. In the end, whilst I loved my Mother, I couldn't understand why alcohol was such a huge factor in her life. Ironically my own family would think the same thing about me in years to come.

Out of all of my brothers, I suppose I was closest to Matthew growing up, due to there being just a year between us. As Matthew was slightly older than me he was the one who introduced me to new things and took me out with him. Throughout our school years Matthew was popular, he was one of the main boys, always the centre of attention and never without a pretty girl on his arm. At the time I was his snotty nosed kid brother but he took me everywhere and because of that we developed a strong bond.

Matthew wasn't a bad footballer either and he used to play in the same junior team as Craig Bellamy. In all honesty Matthew was probably a better footballer than me but he liked the girls and partying too much. He didn't have the real desire needed to make it as a professional.

I also had a good relationship with my two stepbrothers, Daryl and David. David would take me to watch Cardiff City as a youngster and I suppose going to those games first got me interested in football, even though I can't really remember anything about them.

It's funny that David is so interested in football as he can't play at all. I remember he played one game in goal and when he dived he hit his head against the post and knocked himself out. That pretty much sums up his talent for the game.

Daryl, on the other hand, was the one who would let Matthew and me have a sneaky drink when we were growing up. We always thought he was cool for letting us do that. David isn't the best at football but Daryl is shocking, he's completely un-coordinated.

You can tell that David and Daryl are from my Dad's first marriage as athletically they are hilarious. My Dad didn't have an athletic bone in his body, and made me laugh. Some days we went to Tredegar Park and I would challenge him to a race and always beat him, even when I was small. His dancing was also shocking, he had absolutely no rhythm but he used to love bopping anyway.

My Mum was quite the opposite. She had been a very promising young athlete as a teenager. She used to run the 100 metres and my old PE teacher, Mr Richards, who taught my Mum as well, told me she was rapid. Lynn Davies, who featured in the 1964 Olympics, coached my Mum and he thought she could have gone to the Olympics herself. That was until she started going out and enjoying herself and then any dreams she had of competing professionally soon disappeared.

A few years after I was born my parents added my brother Michael to the family. Growing up I was closer to Matthew but when I started playing football seriously my bond with Michael grew. He absolutely loves the game, his knowledge of it is frightening, he's like an encyclopaedia. Michael's not a bad player either, perhaps not good enough to make it as a professional, but certainly a tidy player.

Nathan was born not long after Michael and he was the unfortunate one in the family. He was born with Perthes' disease, a condition that causes the hips to crumble. In his early years he was confined to a wheelchair and we all had to help him. It was tough on him and I remember he had a nasty accident where he fell down the stairs and smashed his head through a glass pane in the living room door. He didn't seem to have any luck and I think those experiences have scarred him a bit as he's got older.

Whilst Nathan's condition was sad, it did provide the family with the opportunity to buy a new car. Before Nathan was born my Dad drove a crap old Ford Escort Estate. It must have been 20 years old even back then but through Nathan's disability, we were given a car allowance so my Dad bought a brand new Escort. We felt like royalty having a new car in our driveway and I'm sure we were the envy of the street. I can still see my Dad driving it now, thinking he was posh in his new car. He didn't have many luxuries in life but this car was one of them. There's absolutely no doubt about it, though, that he would have given that car up in a shot if it meant Nathan could have been cured. Dad was so family orientated; he would do anything for us.

Having had four boys my Mum was desperate to have a daughter so she was over the moon when she gave birth to my sister Sacha in 1990. Sacha was brought up like a little princess, my Mum and Dad doted on her and she had six older brothers looking out for her as well. The problem was that as she was the only girl in the house she needed her own bedroom so Matthew,

Michael, Nathan and me had double bunk beds in one room whilst she had a room to herself.

Our bedroom was unbelievably cramped with the four of us squashed in but we didn't complain. It's fair to say we all loved Sacha, no one resented her and it was nice having a girl around the place. She was a cute girl as well; she had this lovely tight little afro as a kid and everyone used to comment on how gorgeous she was.

When my two step-brothers were with us there were nine of us living in the house, so mealtimes could be hectic. But when my Mum was in a fit state to cook, her meals were always amazing. Because there were so many of us my Mum had to do meals in two sittings, she would be slaving away at the stove all day. In fact it's no wonder sometimes she couldn't face cooking!

It was a given in our house that Saturday night was bolognese night and Sunday afternoons would be roast dinner. Bolognese night was wicked; I used to look forward to it all week. The whole family would sit down, talk about our week and have a good laugh. We were all close and I used to enjoy us all being together and the bolognese my Mum cooked was always immense.

Sunday roasts were amazing as well. Our house was opposite the playing field of Bryn Hafod Primary School so we were out on that field all day, in all sorts of weather, and then my Mum would call us all in for food. Some days it was freezing outside so I would race inside for my roast dinner to warm me up and then watch the football on TV.

It always used to confuse me that whilst we all dug into our food my Mum rarely ate with us. She always claimed she was too tired from cooking to eat and I never thought to question it at the time but through my own troubles with alcohol addiction I know now that when you're drinking you hardly touch food.

A day that the whole family eagerly anticipated each month was family allowance day. On a Monday, once a month, my Mum collected her family allowance money and then spent some of it on little treats for the family. We had fresh sandwiches, cakes, doughnuts and so on. She really went to town and spoilt us. Nowadays most kids think a desert is standard with every meal but back then we honestly could only afford to have dessert once a month and when we did it was a big deal.

There's no doubt about it, times could be tough. I don't want anyone to think we were the poorest family around, because we weren't, but there were times when we were on the breadline. We certainly didn't have the money to buy flash new things, and eating out at a restaurant, or going on holidays were expensive luxuries that weren't an option. Danny Smith was one of my best mates growing up and he always seemed to get the latest stuff for his birthday. I knew we couldn't afford those kind of things and whereas he might get the latest trainers mine would come from Splott Market.

If I did need a new pair of trainers, because mine were ruined, we couldn't go straight out and buy them. I would tell my old man that I needed a new pair and he would say, 'Give me two weeks' and he would save up the money to get them. They certainly wouldn't be any name brands such as Nike or Adidas either; I was lucky to get Ascot. When I got new trainers I had to make them last as my Dad couldn't afford to buy me another pair for a long time. One time I had a pair of Ascot trainers for around three years and in the end they were falling apart but I had to make do.

My Dad hardly ever bought anything with a receipt. I swear! Everything would be from the market or off someone knocking on the door selling stuff. Every couple of weeks 'The Jeans Man', who sold jeans out of his boot, came to our house. He never sold well known brands, but they were jeans nevertheless, and at £8.00 a pair they were all that we could afford.

Some of the guys in the area, who went tea leafing, would also bring the stuff that they had 'acquired' up to our house to see if we were interested. It may not have been strictly legal but buying items off them was the only way that my parents could afford to clothe the family. Including my parents, there were nine of us to feed and clothe in the house on only £140.00 a week. I don't know how my parents did it; it's a miracle really. You don't realise at the time how hard it must have been to survive but now I'm older I really appreciate that what my Mum and Dad did was incredible.

Through one of the guys who had been tea leafing I managed to buy a pair of trainers I had wanted for months, Nike Air Jordans! They were white with black all around the front and I remember seeing the rapper, Tupac Shakur, first wear them and I thought they were slick. I was absolutely desperate for them but they were £100.00 in the shops, close to my Dad's weekly wage, so there was no way we could afford them. Luckily for me a guy knocked on the door selling some trainers and he had the Jordans, I begged my Mum to buy them for me and bless her, she did. I thought I was absolute chocolate walking round in them, if I could have eaten myself I would. My Mum could see how much I wanted them and I don't think I have ever treasured anything as much as I did those trainers.

One of my close mates growing up was a guy called Gareth Williams who lived around the corner from me. He'll kill me for saying this but one of the reasons we became mates was because I fancied his sister. I told him this a few years ago, after we had a few drinks, and I don't think he was too pleased. Despite this Gareth is still one of my closest mates to this day.

Seeing all these guys pick up amazing things like Nike trainers, through tea leafing, set Gareth and me thinking about doing a bit of shop lifting ourselves. Firstly, to wet our lips, we went to Tesco's and stole pairs of boat shoes. We literally grabbed them and ran as quickly out of the store as we could. It was almost too easy.

Feeling confident after our hit on Tesco's we devised a plan to raid ToysRus. We had seen this amazing football box set, which had a football top, shorts, socks, shin pads, ball and boots, and we were determined to have it. We planned our raid with military precision but it basically consisted of us walking in the shop, grabbing the gear and legging it. Incredibly we didn't get caught and we thought we were the next Kray twins.

I went straight home, put on my new gear, and was about to rush out to meet up with Gareth when I heard my old man accusingly say, 'Where did you get all that stuff from?' I panicked and told him that Gareth had a spare set and that he had given it to me. There was no fooling my Dad though, he saw right through me. 'No he didn't', he shouted, 'Tell me where you got it from'.

I started getting defensive and told him, 'Ring Gareth, he'll tell you!' but I knew the game was up. Eventually my old man got it out of me and I told him the whole story.

I couldn't believe it when he dragged me out of the house and took me to Rumney Police Station. He even told me I was going to jail and I wouldn't see the family again. I was absolutely shitting myself; I was only 11. I cried and begged him not to take me but he said it was for my own good. When we got to the station the police gave me a rollicking but they let me off. I think my old man must have had a word with them beforehand but it taught me a hell of a lesson. From that day on I never really got into trouble as a kid. My mates still did a bit of shoplifting but I was too terrified to even think of joining in. It goes to show the kind of man my Dad was, genuine and honest to a fault.

With my Dad having little money to spare, and my shoplifting days at an end, I was forced to do a variety of jobs if I wanted to be able to buy anything. Yet whatever I earned I still had to put some of my wages into the family pot, as did my brothers and sister whenever they picked up some work. As with most kids one of my first jobs was a paper round but that didn't last too long as I dumped the papers in the woods instead of delivering them. Daryl and David asked me to help them out on the building sites from time to time and that was bloody hard work but kept me in shape. One job I remember was laying tarmac at a gypsy site when I was about 13, it was a good laugh in all honesty and the gypsies treated me well.

A time of year that we all enjoyed in the Roberts household was Christmas, even though it must have been a struggle for my Mum and Dad as they would have to buy gifts for seven kids. Whilst we never got any expensive presents, the ones that we did get we treasured. I remember that my favourite present was a football and that probably gave me more pleasure than anything else could have. When I see what my own kids get for Christmas I think that they don't need loads of expensive things, like computer consoles, to be happy.

We absolutely loved the festive period in our house but it wasn't just the presents we looked forward to. My Mum would order a huge hamper every year that literally had everything you can think of in it, pies, jams, cakes, pickled onions and so on. It was delivered a week before Christmas and Matthew and me couldn't wait to see what was in it. We weren't allowed to eat any of it before Christmas though, no matter how much we begged, but we still took great pride in taking everything out and presenting it like you saw in the catalogue.

One of the things I cherished most about Christmas was that we were all together as a family. As I said before, we were all close, and not only would we all have time off school but my Dad was off as well and we loved having him with us.

Music was always a big thing in our house growing up. My Mum was always playing UB40, Marvin Gaye or anything by Motown Records on the record player, although her big love was Queen and Freddy Mercury. She was absolutely mad on him. I'll never forget the day that Freddy died. My Mum had coincidentally been playing Queen records all day and when she heard the news she was convinced that Freddy had been trying to make a connection with her. She must have been drinking at the time!

Through my Mum's love of music I began to develop a passion for it myself, although my tastes were a little different. It's funny, even though I can't remember how

I got into football, I can vividly remember the day I first heard music by Tupac Shakur, the famous American rap artist. My mate Lee Colville was listening to something on his Walkman during break time at school and he said, 'Here you go Chris, check this out', and handed me his headphones. I put them on and was absolutely blown away; I had never heard anything like it. The song was 'Dear Mama' by Tupac and everything about it appealed to me, the music, the lyrics, the passion, it was all so raw and heartfelt.

From that day on I started to get into hip-hop, which then progressed to jungle and garage music. I even started to DJ now and again at the local youth club. The only problem was that we weren't allowed to play any hip-hop, due to all the swearing, so that counted Tupac out. It was okay though as I used to play a bit of Boyz II Men and R Kelly in an attempt to woo the girls. It's fair to say that it didn't always work but I thought I was cool anyway.

As with most boys, girls were a massive part of my life as a teenager. My brother Matthew was the real playboy in the family though, I wasn't in his league, but I did alright for myself. My first girlfriend was called Natalie Davies, who I met at Bryn Hafod Primary School when I was 10. She was from a mixed parentage background, like me, and looked a bit like Whitney Houston. I thought she was gorgeous. Looking back we had a nice little relationship; we would hang out at each other's houses and have a kiss and we would even buy each other little gifts. For instance I remember she once bought me a Puma t-shirt, which I wore all the time, and I saved up to buy her a peso ring.

Following primary school we both went on to

Llanrumney High School and stayed together for a few years. The relationship ended when she moved to the other side of Cardiff and met a guy with a car. How could I compete? I had a Magnum pushbike so there was only ever going to be one winner there.

After Natalie I started to see a girl called Gemma Evans who was one of the best looking girls in school. I thought I had a right result when we got together. Our relationship was definitely a love-hate one though. One minute we were all over each other and then the next we were rowing in class and the teacher had to get involved. She was a good girl and we were really into each other for a bit.

I had one relationship that ended in tragedy. Throughout primary school I had been close to a girl called Claire Draine. She was a lovely looking girl and had a wicked personality, which made her one of the most popular kids in school. We were close friends, and whilst we both fancied each other, the relationship never went any further than that.

When I was about 13 I went to a Valentines disco at the youth club and there were loads of rumours that Claire had been rushed to hospital and had died. I refused to believe them but then my worst fears were confirmed when I found out that she had an asthma attack and had passed away. Claire was one of my closest friends, and we had spent a lot of time together, so for her suddenly to be gone tore me apart. It doubled my grief when her Mum found a rose that she was going to give to me at the disco. When the local paper got hold of the story there was a picture of me in it, holding the rose, looking devastated. Losing her left a big hole in my life, as if a ray of sunshine had disappeared forever.

I like to think I was popular in school. I suppose I was an outgoing kid, in fact I was probably a genuine mad little tearaway. It wasn't that I was naughty but I was full of energy and that seemed to attract people to me. No doubt my football also did a lot of talking for me—an aspect of my life that would soon consume everything that I did.

2

GETTING INTO FOOTBALL

I suppose my earliest memory of playing football was when I was eight years old and my mates and me used to mess around with a ball on the playground of Bryn Hafod Primary School. We played a bit of rugby now and then as well and I found I was quite good at it, in part due to my pace. I was a bit like Forrest Gump, sprinting past everyone without having a clue about the rules. I remember in one game that I played for the school, I picked up the ball and bombed my way past the whole team for what would have been an unbelievable try. Unfortunately I forgot to put the ball down and ran straight over the dead ball line!

My rugby playing days soon ended when everyone started getting bigger than me and if they did manage to catch me I would get crippled. I wasn't too keen on that aspect of the game so I decided to stick to football.

In the school playground I was always one of the better players but wanted to start playing in some proper games so when a few of my mates joined the local junior team, Caer Castell, I tagged along. During that first season at Caer Castell the manager played me up front and I was on fire. I must have been around 10 at the time and everything I hit went in. I think I scored over 70 goals in my first season but unbelievably I can't remember any of them.

Word soon spread throughout the community that I was a promising footballer and a guy called Malcolm, who was the local butcher, offered me various incentives to encourage me. If I scored one goal he gave me a sausage, if I scored two he gave me a burger and if I scored a hat trick he gave me a steak. If I scored more than three, which I did quite regularly, he would give me lots of different meats to take home and feed the family. My family treated me like a hero when I walked through the door with enough food for everyone; it was a huge treat.

The one game that I can vividly recall from that first season is the Cup Final. It was played at Sophia Gardens, in Cardiff. We won 8–1 and I scored five! Without being big headed I was shit hot that day and I knew it. Everything I tried came off and I was shooting from everywhere.

After collecting my winner's trophy I ran over to my old man, who watched every game that I played, to see what he thought about my display. As I walked up to him I saw that he was surrounded by a few guys and they were all deep in conversation. I didn't think much of it at the time, I thought that they may be other parents or something like that. Once my old man had finished speaking to them he turned to me and said in a surprised, but proud, voice, 'I've just had scouts from Luton, Norwich and Cardiff all ask if they can take you on trial'.

I didn't even know anything about scouts back then, all I thought about was playing and scoring goals. The idea that I could actually go to a professional club, at such a young age, was news to me. As soon as I heard that news from my Dad my heart literally popped out of my chest. I won the cup, played out of my skin and suddenly I had professional clubs after me. It was the perfect day and one that I will never forget. It certainly set me on my way.

Following that final things literally went berserk, we had scouts from all over the country ringing the house, turning up at my games and sending me letters. It was mental! I had offers from everywhere and for a time it seemed that Dad and me would spend all our time in his Ford Escort travelling the country checking out the different clubs.

The first trial that I went to was at Luton Town. Their scout, Cyril Beech, is well known in South Wales and he had arranged for me to spend a week in Luton training with their youth team. Looking back now it seems nuts, I was 11 years old and I was put on a train at Cardiff Central Station, alone, to make my way up to Luton. It was the first time I had left South Wales so it was almost like a little holiday for me, I didn't have a clue what to expect but I was excited.

When I finally arrived in Luton, in one piece, I was picked up at the station and taken to Kenilworth Road. The other trialists, including me, were taken into the first team changing room where we were greeted by the apprentices, who were all aged between 16 and 18. They sat in the corner scoping us out and they seemed huge, I was shit scared of them to be honest.

One of the apprentices was a young John Hartson who was coming through the ranks at the time. Someone mentioned to John that I was Welsh and I think he was expected to look after me but he didn't seem that interested. To be fair, as a young lad the last thing you want to do is look after some kid on trial and John kept his distance.

We were shown around the stadium and even back then I can remember thinking that the place was a shit hole. They took us into an old gymnasium, at the back of one of the stands, where we watched the first team and YTS boys practising their heading by jumping up and heading a ball attached to a piece of string. The gym was minging, it stank of mould and was freezing cold.

Despite all that I thoroughly enjoyed my time at Luton. We trained every day and the family I stayed with looked after me really well. It was my first taste of life at a professional club and I loved it. When the week was done they asked me to return in my school holidays but I had already committed to spend time at another club.

It seemed that every weekend and school holiday I had I would spend at a different club. I didn't care though, I got to play football and have a little trip away from Cardiff as well. My Dad always encouraged me to see as many clubs as possible, not only so I could gain some experience, but also because it was my only opportunity to see places other than my home town.

I went up to Norwich for a bit, which was where Craig Bellamy was playing, but it felt like the other side of the world up there so I decided not to go back. Cardiff, Stoke and Southampton were all showing real interest in me and I loved those clubs. At one point I was playing in the schoolboy teams for all three and doing really well. In particular, I loved going to Southampton as I stayed in an army base for a week. As a young kid being around all the army stuff was unreal. In fact I think I was more into the army base than the football.

As they were my hometown team I spent most of my time playing for Cardiff but the head of youth development, Gavin Tait, was always happy to let me go off and see other clubs. Sheffield United, Sheffield Wednesday, Glasgow Rangers, Spurs and Leeds were all sniffing around and I wanted a taste of them all.

Everything seemed to be going so well but then disaster struck. I was playing for the Cardiff Schools team and as I went into a challenge I wrenched my knee. I instantly felt intense pain shoot up my leg and fell into a crumpled heap on the pitch. There was no way that I could continue to play so I was carried off in absolute agony. In the car on the way home my knee was throbbing and I was crying to my Dad, 'It's killing me Dad, I've done something bad'.

The next day Dad rang Gavin Tait at Cardiff City and told him what had happened. Gavin got the physio to look at me at the club straight away but he couldn't initially diagnose the problem.

After that I was sent to see a few specialists, and continued having physio, but no one seemed able to sort out my knee. For the next year I hardly kicked a ball. The few times I tried I had to stop after a few minutes as my knee locked up or gave way. It was a depressing time, the one thing that I loved doing, and excelled at, I couldn't do. I suppose it was during this time away from football that I really started to get into my music and motorbikes.

Bikes were a huge obsession for me at one point. I was desperate to have one, and would beg my Dad, but he wasn't having any of it. Nothing fascinated me more than watching people riding bikes. During a game I remember that someone was riding a bike on the pitch opposite us and I stopped playing so that I could watch. I thought they were the height of coolness and I would have done anything to get one.

When I was 14 my Dad finally got me out of my obsession with bikes by letting me drive his car in the car park at Llanrumney High School. For some reason, after that, I was more interested in cars than bikes which is probably a good thing as riding a bike as a professional footballer isn't the best thing you can do, as Carlo Cudicini, the Spurs goalkeeper, found to his cost recently. Although now I'm retired I fancy getting my motorbike licence and giving it a go.

After occupying myself with music and bikes, a scan of my knee finally revealed that I had torn my cartilage. I had an operation where two thirds of the cartilage was removed from my knee and that seemed to do the trick. Whilst I was soon back playing the injury would have serious repercussions later on in my career.

Within six weeks of the operation I was back kicking a ball, which was probably too soon. I hadn't even had any rehab but I was so desperate to play that I didn't care. It was weird being back at first; I found it a lot harder to twist and turn and for some reason I didn't seem to be as quick as I was before the injury.

My confidence was low and this started to affect my game. It took me a long time to work out what I could and couldn't do and adjust accordingly.

Despite still suffering, and feeling that I wasn't back to my best, the biggest club in the world, Manchester United, offered me a trial. Opportunities like that don't come along everyday and even though I didn't feel anywhere near fully fit I was determined to give it a shot.

The trial consisted of a match on a Wednesday night with lots of other kids trying to make an impression. Manchester United and Scottish international, Brian McClair, was present and I remember being excited at seeing him. At this time he was still in the Manchester United first team and was quite a big name.

Unfortunately the game seemed to pass me by. My lack of fitness and confidence told, and I didn't have one of my better games, so it was of no surprise that I wasn't invited back. I was gutted but knew in the back of my mind, even before the game, that I would struggle to play my best under the circumstances.

Every now and again I see the Manchester United scout who spotted me and he always says to me that the knee injury 'lost you a yard of pace and it cost you'. As a professional I was always regarded as being quick but that injury definitely curtailed my speed. Sometimes I do think that if I hadn't suffered that injury my career could have been different. Don't get me wrong, I had a good career, one that I'm proud of, but that extra yard of pace may have seen me play at a higher level.

The staff at Cardiff City were all brilliant towards

me as I recovered from my injury. Gavin Tait, and coach Gwynn Williams, were always asking how I was and Jimmy Goodfellow, who had suffered a similar problem with his knee in the past, also gave me advice as to how to manage the pain, 'Always keep the knee warm Chris' he used to say.

Stoke City were also good to me and kept asking me to go up there even when I wasn't playing so well. It's fair to say that at this time I felt I owed both Cardiff and Stoke a lot and I tried to play as often as I could for both teams but the time came when I had to make a difficult decision between them.

When I was 14 the two clubs both offered me a four year contract, consisting of two years as a schoolboy and two years on their Youth Training Scheme as an apprentice. It was a difficult decision and I was torn about where I wanted to go, as I loved the staff at both clubs. Some days I was set to sign for Stoke and then other days it would be Cardiff.

In the end my old man, who as I got older I had christened 'Pops', helped make my mind up for me. We were driving up Rumney Hill when he asked me, 'So Chris, what are you going to do?'

It was one of those days when I fancied Stoke so I said to him, 'I'm going to Stoke I think'. As I said it I looked at him for a reaction and he seemed a little taken back. For a brief moment I swear I saw his eyes fill up slightly as well. It may have been the cold, as I never saw Pops cry, but he genuinely looked upset. We had both been through so much together and by now we were like best mates. He had watched all my games, and travelled around the country with me, and I think the thought of me leaving Cardiff must have upset him. After seeing his reaction I made a snap decision, 'I'm only joking, I'm going to sign for Cardiff'.

This seemed to lift him but he still said, 'You sign for whoever you want, don't worry about me'. But my mind was made up by then, I realised that I didn't want to be away from my Dad.

Another factor in my decision was that I had been with Cardiff since I was 11 years old, not only had they always been good to me but I also liked all the coaches and was friendly with all the players. In fact one of my best friends, Nathan 'Shaper' Cadette, had also been offered a YTS contract at Cardiff, so that helped make my mind up.

Shaper and me first met when we were both playing for Cardiff Schools. I was still playing for my club team, Caer Castell, whilst he was playing for a team called Pentwyn Dynamos. Everyone who has played junior football in Cardiff knows that Pentwyn are regarded as the Real Madrid of junior football. They always attract the best players and seem to win everything. You can also always guarantee that there will be plenty of scouts at Pentwyn games so they were definitely regarded as the team to play for in the area.

As a result I always fancied going to Pentwyn and one day Shaper asked why I didn't sign up. I told him I was keen so he said he would speak to his manager, Malcolm Frazer, about me. Malcolm was the league's equivalent of Sir Alex Ferguson, everyone in football circles in Cardiff knows him and he is a hell of a character.

Malcolm had earned his nickname 'Malcolm the

Mountie, he always gets his man' due to attracting the top players to Pentwyn. I swear that within a few hours of Shaper telling Malcolm I was interested in playing for him he was round my house signing me up.

Making my debut for Pentwyn was as nerve racking as any football experience I have had. Getting the call up for them was like being asked to play at a top club. I vividly remember sitting in the changing room at Pentwyn Leisure Centre, before my first game, wondering whether I could even break into the team, then Malcolm threw me the number 9 shirt and I knew I was in. I was ecstatic.

During my time at Pentwyn I must have averaged 40 goals a season, despite not playing in all the games due to being away with Cardiff or Stoke or on trial at other clubs. Due to scoring so many goals I seemed to be in the *Football Echo* every week and I loved seeing my name in print, it made me feel famous. I'm gutted I didn't keep any of the newspaper cuttings from back then as I would love to look at them now and reminisce.

People like Malcolm amaze me. For over 30 years he has put every spare moment that he has into kids' football. He doesn't get paid for his time nor does he expect to get any recognition, he just loves it. Hundreds of kids over the years have had a happier childhood thanks to Malcolm. He has also been responsible for grooming a number of professional players through the Pentwyn youth system such as former Cardiff, Wigan and Tranmere Rovers player, Simon Howarth. Without a shadow of a doubt Malcolm Frazer is Cardiff junior football! It sometimes annoys me to see celebrities receive awards and honours for doing their (well paid) job, yet Malcolm gets no recognition. If anyone deserved an honour in this country he would be the first name on my list.

My Pentwyn days were happy ones and Shaper and me built up a great partnership on the pitch. He usually played midfield and I played up front and our friendship helped us develop a telepathic understanding which led to Shaper setting up a number of my goals. At Cardiff City, Gavin Tait absolutely loved the two of us; we were his golden boys and that gave us even more confidence. I was certain that one day we would recreate our partnership in the Cardiff City first team.

Another one of my good mates growing up was Leon Jeanne, who of course went on to play for Queens Park Rangers and Cardiff City before falling victim to drug and alcohol addiction. I met him on his first day of school at Bryn Hafod Primary School and we have been mates ever since. I was in the year above him and I remember Leon coming in with his Mum and I was asked to look after him. The two of us hit it off straight away, we were inseparable.

Whilst we were both into the same type of things, our friendship really flourished over our love for football. Sadly our careers took different paths but ironically we both fell victim to addiction in different forms. Growing up Leon was an unbelievable talent, by far the most promising young player in Cardiff and in all honesty probably Wales, if not all of the UK. He was a phenomenon! All the big clubs were chasing him and I fully expected him to become a mega star.

I'll make a big statement here but I truly believe it, on the basis of sheer talent Leon was better than Craig Bellamy.

For as long as I live I will never forget the time we both played for Wales Under 21s against Belarus together, he was untouchable that night. Their defenders couldn't handle him and in the end they must have had four players trying to man mark him but he still skinned them all. Out of all the pros I have played with over the years he is still the most talented. The way his career turned out is an absolute tragedy but I know he still harbours dreams of making a comeback and I hope someone gives him a chance as I still think he has some magic left in him.

Even to this day we are still like brothers. He is important to me and I know that if I ever needed anyone to help me he would be there and he knows I would do the same for him. If anything our battles against addiction have only served to make us closer.

Once I told Cardiff I'd decided to sign for them they organised for my family and me to attend a match to sign the contract after the game. The morning before the game I went to Top Man, in the town centre, to buy myself some smart clothes so I would look the part. I was beaming with pride wearing all my flash gear down to Ninian Park.

We went to watch the Welsh derby, Cardiff City v Swansea City and the atmosphere was frightening. When Cardiff scored the Swansea fans started ripping up the chairs and using them as missiles. Both fans started to pile into each other and I saw some guys take an absolute battering. When the game finished we walked down from the director's box to meet the chairman, Rick Wright. As we did so we passed loads of fans receiving medical treatment in the directors lounge as their heads had been split open due to being hit by chairs.

It was all a bit surreal but that didn't stop me putting pen to paper and I eagerly signed the contract I had been offered. I had done it; I was going to be a footballer!

From that moment on I was Mr Football. I ate, drank and slept the game, nothing could compete with it. By the age of 14 a lot of my mates had started to experiment with drink and drugs but I wasn't interested and I focussed on making it at Cardiff. If all my mates were going down to the Eastern Leisure Centre, which is where everyone used to hang out, then I went down with them and maybe had a can or two of beer but that was my limit. The only reason I went there was because it was where all the best looking girls from school were. If I had a game the next day I wouldn't even go out as I made sure I had cleaned my boots, got all my kit together and had an early night. It would, of course, be later in my career that drink got hold of me, but at this point I was obsessed with football.

During my teenage years I watched and played football as much as I could. There was no particular team that I was keen on, I was more a fan of individual players. If I had to say I supported a team it would be Liverpool, purely because my Nan was from there and she bought me the kit.

However, if there was a player I really liked I supported the team that they played for. One year I was an Aston Villa fan purely because I used to love their winger Tony Daley. He was quick and skilful like me and I used to try to base my game on him. Other players I loved watching were Dean Saunders, Ryan Giggs, Mark Hughes, Gazza and Matthew Le Tissier.

For me, one player stood head and shoulders above the rest. That was Ian Wright. I absolutely worshipped the man. He was like a god to me; he seemed to have it all, the skill, the charisma, the personality and an unbelievable enthusiasm for the game.

Wright genuinely appreciated the talent he was given, perhaps because he came into the professional game late after a stint in non-league football. I know he has had some troubles, and was a bit of a kid from time to time, but on the pitch he always seemed to deliver.

I remember the one time I met him, I froze. At the time he was finishing his career at Burnley and I was starting mine at Cardiff. Burnley were coming down to Ninian Park and I was absolutely desperate to be involved. I was coming back from an injury though and hadn't played for a few weeks so it looked as if I would miss out. All week prior to the game I begged the manager, Frank Burrows, to put me in the squad, and I was training my guts out to make it, but in the end he decided against it. I was distraught at being left out and missing the chance to be on the same pitch as my hero.

As luck would have it, Ian wasn't playing that day either but he had travelled down with the squad. For some reason he was a good friend of our goalkeeping coach, George Wood, so before the game the two of them were having a natter in the tunnel at Ninian Park. I stood next to them both, listening to my hero, and trying to think of something to say. I was completely star struck and desperate for his autograph but I bottled it. Every time I was about to ask him I thought that he may think it was weird to have another pro ask so I decided not to do it. It's one of my biggest regrets. In the end I mustered a hello but then nothing else came out. He probably thought I was a right weirdo stood there, staring at him. I have such a high regard for Ian Wright that I even gave my oldest son, Ethan, the middle name 'Ian' after my hero.

Once I had signed for Cardiff my schooling fell by the wayside. I'll admit I wasn't the most intelligent at school anyway, I just didn't have it, but I always tried hard and maybe if I hadn't signed that contract with Cardiff I would have achieved more than the GCSE B grade that I got for PE.

Maths was the one academic subject that I was decent at, until algebra came along, and then I completely lost interest. I also always used to enjoy writing stories in English even though I wasn't particularly good at it. In one class we were asked to write a new soap opera so I had the genius idea to write one called 'WestEnders'. My English teacher, Mrs Hirst, still winds me up about that to this day.

Even though I lost interest in school I still went every single day, I never mitched. My PE teacher, Mr Richards, or Rocko as we called him behind his back, was integral in making sure I stayed on the straight and narrow. We struck a deal where as long as I still went to maths, English and science classes I could spend the rest of my time in the school gym. It was great, I spent all day playing football, table tennis, working out and so on. I didn't mind helping out by cleaning the place or delivering letters for Rocko if he asked me to.

My Mum also played a big part in making sure I went to school. If I told her I wasn't going in she would say, 'Fine but you won't be allowed to play football tonight if you don't go'. That soon grabbed my attention and within minutes I would be putting my school uniform on. If anyone wanted to threaten me as a kid all they had to do was deprive me of football and that would be the ultimate punishment.

From the age of 14, though, I was simply counting the days until I turned 16 and I could finally become a full time footballer.

3

BEST DAYS OF
MY LIFE

I can honestly say that the best years of my life were between the ages of 16–18 when I was an apprentice on the Youth Training Scheme at Cardiff City. Whilst I had to work hard it was great fun and some of my happiest memories come from this time.

All the apprentices were around the same age, constantly wound each other up and acted like idiots to amuse each other. Some of the stuff that went on was mental but when I think back to those days I always have a big smile on my face. It's funny how you really don't appreciate the best times of your life until they are gone.

We had some real characters in my YTS group as well. We were all 16 years old and from different backgrounds, some working class like myself, and others whose parents were wealthy, but we all came together and had a blast. There was Shaper, and me of course, but there was also a guy from the valleys called Jerome Jermiah, who we called JJ, Lee Phillips, Will Hughes, Danny Thomas, Gavin Smith and an absolute gem of a guy everyone called Wedgie. I don't think we ever found out his real name, he was christened Wedgie and that was it, a star was born.

Wedgie used to crack us all up, sometimes when he didn't even mean to. He was a little stumpy guy with a thick Welsh accent and he was shocking at long distance running. Wedgie was always right at the back shouting at us in his funny valley's accent, 'Slow down boys! Slow fucking down you bunch of kiss asses!'

I wasn't the best long distance runner myself, as my body wasn't built for it, my speciality was quick bursts over 10 yards, but I always made sure I ran a few yards ahead of Wedgie so the coaches left me alone and bollocked him instead. He would scream at me, 'You bastard, slow fucking down!'

An average day on the YTS went something like this: I left my house in Llanrumney at around 8.15am so that I could get the bus into town. Once I got into town I had to catch another bus to Sloper Road where I would then make my way to Ninian Park. We had to be changed and ready for duty by 9.30am so if I missed the bus into town I had to leg it all the way to the ground otherwise there would be hell to play.

At 9.30am we sorted out the senior pros before they went off to train. We were definitely the whipping boys for the pros. If they told us to wipe their ass we'd do it with a smile on our faces or they made life hell. We did everything for them and they enjoyed making life as difficult as possible for us.

For instance, we used to train at Jubilee Park, across the road from Ninian Park, and everyone nicknamed it 'Dog Shit Park' because the place was covered in the stuff. Almost every day Carl Dale had me scraping the crap off the bottom of his boots, it used to make me retch.

If we moaned, or didn't perform to the required standard, the pros called a court case. One of them acted as a judge and the rest were the jury whilst the accused had to plead their case as to why they were innocent of the charges. Funnily enough we were almost always given a guilty verdict.

There were two punishments if we were found guilty; either lights out in the changing room or lights out in the boot room. Lights out in the changing room consisted of someone turning the lights out for 30 seconds while the pros tried to beat the living daylights out of us. The only hope was to evade capture until the lights came back on as if they got hold of us they would beat us black and blue.

Lights out in the boot room was even worse. It was the same as in the changing room but everyone had boots and wet towels in their hands and they would either whip us with the towels or launch boots at our heads. A number of the pros were in their 30s but were still like big kids. That's the great thing about being a footballer; you don't have to grow up.

The big characters in the first team at this time were Lee Jarman, Simon Haworth and Scott Young. They were always giving out banter and up to no good but we all looked up to them. They were all Welsh boys, like us, who had gone through the YTS system at Cardiff and reached the first team.

The pros that I mainly looked after were Tony Elliot, Haydn Fleming and Kevin Lloyd. Every morning before I arrived at Ninian Park I had to buy a newspaper for Tony. He gave me a fiver a week to do this and as I was only earning £218.00 a month as a trainee I was eager to earn extra money any way that I could. Kevin Lloyd also helped me out in giving me £2.00 for every goal that I scored. It acted as a great incentive and helped me earn an extra couple of quid as well.

My monthly wage never lasted very long. I gave my Dad £50 for keep and usually bought some clothes, such as a YSL shirt or a pair of trainers. I spent the rest of my money on a few nights out on the town and then I would be skint again. I considered myself rich, though, as it was still more money than I had ever had in my pocket.

An episode that illustrates how tight money was for me was when *Soccer AM*'s Helen Chamberlain came to Ninian Park to watch Torquay United play Cardiff. After the game Helen asked if someone could give her directions back to the motorway, as she was afraid she would get lost. I volunteered to accompany her, as my house in Llanrumney was near the M4. However, the real reason for my generous offer was that I was supposed to be meeting my mates in town and I couldn't afford the bus fare. I therefore directed Helen into the town centre, quickly gave her directions to the motorway, and then jumped out. Poor Helen, she was probably driving around Cardiff for hours whilst I partied away.

After we had sorted out the pros we did everything and anything that we were told to do. We were all given different jobs; some were in charge of cleaning the showers, others the changing room. I used to run the tearoom and I like to think I ran a tight ship. It was shit hot. Some of the boys were obviously jealous of how well I was doing in the tearoom as they were constantly trying to stitch me up. They would put my tea bags in the urinals or hide my cups. I went mad but it only made things worse. It was all banter and I always got my own back.

It seems crazy now to think that as young trainee footballers we were cleaning toilets but that's the way it was back then and it definitely kept our feet on the ground. There were no egos in any of us and if we got too big for our boots, numerous people brought us crashing back down to earth.

Whilst it sounds like life on the YTS was a never-ending chore of looking after the pros we did occasionally get to play football. Once we had finished our YTS jobs we trained and then after training we would break for lunch. More often than not we spent the afternoon working on our ball skills or hitting the weights.

Once we got home we had to immediately wash our training gear as we only had one set. These days the kids at the Academy have fresh kit every day, which is cleaned in the laundry room at the club, but if we turned up in dirty kit, or without it, then we received a dressing down.

If we weren't training at Dog Shit Park then Gwynn Williams and Gavin Tait had us playing on the gravel car park across the road from Ninian Park or we were running up and down the stairs of the Grand Stand in the stadium itself. We had no other facilities to train at so we had to make do. Looking back it seems nuts now that this was where professional footballers had to train but no one really thought anything of it.

Travelling to away games used to be a nightmare for us as well. We had a little down and out G registration white mini bus, which somehow took us all over the country without breaking down. Games at places like

Plymouth were a real pain in the ass as kick off was at 11.00am and we had to be there by 9.45am. Consequently we had to set off at the crack of dawn. Not only was the bus tiny, so we were all crammed in together, but also it had no heating, so on a cold day we were all freezing. We virtually lived in that bus, I remember one time we actually all slept in it as well. It was pure survival but those types of experiences made us even closer as a group.

During my first YTS year the joint managers of the first team were Kenny Hibbitt and Russell Osman. Kenny had been a legend at Wolves as a player where he had enjoyed a career going on 16 years. Russell, on the other hand, had not only had a great career with Ipswich Town and England but he had also starred in the film, *Escape to Victory*, alongside Pele, Michael Caine and Sylvester Stallone. It was a real thrill for the youngsters at Cardiff to have two former players, who had done so much in the game, in charge. If we ever received a compliment from either of them it would make us feel 100 feet tall.

During that first year as an apprentice I felt that I did quite well. I was scoring regularly and had an excellent end of year review from Gavin Tait. At the end of the season Gavin even said to me, 'Don't go mad in the summer, keep fit and you may get a chance in the first team next year'. Unfortunately he didn't know that I had already booked a two-week holiday, with the rest of the YTS boys, to Ibiza. He would have gone mad if he had known.

Those two weeks in Ibiza were mental. Ten of the YTS boys went, including Shaper, and for many of us it was the first time that we had been abroad. The mixture of an abundance of sun and alcohol, and girls wearing next to nothing, was appealing to a group of young men and we lapped it all up.

The first four days were utter carnage, we hardly slept and it was a non-stop party. I don't think there was a moment during those four days when any of us were sober and I was completely out of my head on drink the whole time. Me, and one of the other YTS boys, Will Hughes, would still be hammered at six in the morning, as we ate a full fry up from one of the local cafés, before we would get straight back on it. One time Will was so wrecked he fell asleep, head first, into his breakfast and had baked beans all over his face. Thinking about that, even now, still makes me laugh.

All the boys seemed to hook up with girls and I was no different. In the first couple of days I met a girl called Karen from Manchester and I tried hard to impress her. One afternoon we hired mopeds and I was driving mine around San Antonio, off my skull, thinking I was an absolute legend.

For some reason, when we got back to our hotel, I thought to myself, 'Do you know what, me riding this moped through the hotel would go down well here', so that's exactly what I did and I ended up crashing it into the bar. I was so far gone with alcohol that I staggered up from the wreckage, went to my room and collapsed on the bed into a deep sleep.

The next thing I knew I heard a loud banging at the door, I thought it was one of the boys winding me up so I kept yelling, 'Piss off!' The knocking became louder and whoever it was wouldn't go away, I was fuming. I leapt out of bed and opened the door, about to kick off, only to be greeted by the hotel owner and security. They started going crazy at me in Spanish and I didn't have a clue what was going on as I had completely forgotten about my accident with the moped. They dragged me downstairs and showed me the state of the bar with the moped still in the middle of it. It suddenly all came flooding back to me and I thought, 'Shit, I'm in trouble here'.

The owner, unsurprisingly, kicked me out of the hotel and for a time I thought I was going to have to sleep on the beach for the rest of the holiday, but thankfully the tour operator sorted me out with alternative accommodation. My new accommodation was a fleapit but I suppose that was the least I deserved after what I had done. I could easily have been arrested and thrown in jail, which would have had Gavin Tait raging if he had found out.

We hit it so hard during those first few days that I spent every penny that I had with me so I had to ring home and beg my Dad to put more cash into my bank account. I don't think he was too impressed but bless him he did it. It was a good job I ran so low on the money front as it meant I couldn't continue the ridiculous sessions I had been having. In the second week the drinking was nowhere near as hardcore and I started going on long runs to try to get myself into some sort of shape.

We flew back to Cardiff on a Sunday night and I think it was the same night Mike Tyson chewed Evander Holyfield's ear off. We got home in the early evening, grabbed some sleep and then had to report for the start of pre-season training in the morning. Those first few days of pre-season were rough on all the YTS lads as we hadn't exactly had good preparation for it and still had a lot of alcohol and fried breakfasts to run out of our systems. After the first week we were okay but those first couple of days were hell.

Thankfully the tales of our tour in Ibiza never got back to the club and as far as Gavin Tait was concerned I had been a model pro all summer . . . if only he knew the half of it!

Nowadays the YTS is all but dead and it has, by and large, been replaced by the academy system, which I suppose is a more professional approach to developing young footballers. The academies are excellent in that regard but I really don't believe that they teach young players how to be a man and remain humble. We didn't have anything handed to us on a plate; we had to work for it. A lot of these young kids are already earning hundreds of thousands of pounds a year and they haven't done anything in the game. I bet that if you told them to clean the toilets half of them would tell you where to go. The game has definitely changed, some of it for the better, some of it for the worse but I wouldn't swap my days as a trainee for anything else in the world.

4

HIGHS AND LOWS

During the start of the second year of my YTS it was obvious that Mum and Pops were having problems, I suspect due to her drinking. In the end they separated and decided to get divorced. I was obviously upset because no one likes to see their family ripped apart but it had been on the cards for a while and I can't say that I was all that surprised.

Football wise I started where I had left off the previous season and scored four goals in my first four games. Any dreams that I harboured of playing for the first team at this time still seemed a long way off. It wasn't that the first team were playing all that well but there was a Cardiff City legend in Carl Dale in front of me, as well as Kevin Nugent.

However, early into the season Carl Dale picked up an injury and then Kevin Nugent got a knock in the following game so the team was short on fit forwards. The club brought in Chris Greenacre on loan and even with a bit of an injury crisis I never thought for one moment that I was anywhere near the first team picture as by this stage I hadn't even played a game for the reserves.

One Friday, in mid-September, I was doing a rush job, cleaning the referee's room, so that I could get away early, and have a wander around town, when, as I was finishing up, Russell Osman, Kenny Hibbitt and Gavin Tait walked in and shut the door behind them. Initially I panicked and thought, 'Shit, what have I done wrong?' Everything I had done over the past week ran through my mind and I thought, 'I went out last Saturday but it was a relatively quiet one, I've been training hard and playing well. My diet's good. What the hell have I done?'

I looked at Kenny Hibbitt and said as innocently as possible, 'What's wrong Ken?'

'No, it's gaffer to you,' he instantly barked back. There was no doubt now in my mind, I was in deep shit. Out of nowhere the next thing he said to me was, 'How many tickets do you want for tomorrow?'

I couldn't work him out so for a while I stared at him blankly and finally muttered 'Why?' pretty sure a nasty twist in the tale was on its way.

'You're involved against Rochdale tomorrow. How many tickets do you need for your family?' he casually replied as if it was something I should have been expecting.

I didn't know what to say or do. I must have looked a prize idiot as I stared at him with my mouth gaping for a good few seconds, still sure it was a wind up.

Russell snapped, 'Don't take the mickey. How many tickets do you need?'

A figure jumped into my head so I blurted out, 'Ten'.

Russell left the referees room, went into the front office and came back with 10 tickets, which he proceeded to hand over to me. Kenny then told me, 'Go home, put your feet up and relax and we'll see you here tomorrow'.

I instantly threw down all my training equipment and ran to find Shaper. I eventually found him cleaning the showers. When I saw him I spilled out the words, 'Shape. I'm involved in the first team tomorrow'.

'Fuck off,' he replied whilst continuing to wipe down the floor. However, when I showed him my 10 tickets for the game, that grabbed his attention. He couldn't believe it but I think he was made up for me.

After telling Shaper, I ran to get the bus back home so I could break the news to my family. The only problem was that when I got home Pops was still at work so I had to wait until 4.00pm to tell him. As soon as he came through the door I shouted, 'Pops, I'm with the first team tomorrow!'

My old man had one of those proud father moments; he was smiling from ear to ear and kept saying to me, 'I always knew you were going to make it'. I was thrilled to see Pops so pleased. Seeing that I had made him so happy doubled my pleasure.

Amongst all the excitement I forgot that I would need to wear a suit and a tie to the game. Years earlier I always thought a former player called Damon Searle looked the business when he went to games in this blue suit jacket and black trousers. I wanted to look the part but the only problem was I didn't actually own a suit. The only suit in the house belonged to Matthew and it was a bright blue monstrosity with a granddad collar. It was shocking but I had no choice, I had to wear it.

The minute I walked into the dressing room the next day the pros hammered me for it. Lee Jarman and Jeff Eckhardt in particular slaughtered me, 'Who the hell do you think you are?' Everyone roasted me from left, right and centre, even the quieter players, who didn't normally pipe up, had a go. I didn't know how to react so I sat down in the corner and tried to keep a low profile, after all my suit was loud enough.

For as long as I live I'll never forget that feeling I had running onto the Ninian Park turf for the warm up as a first team player. I was running out for my hometown team and that had been my goal since I signed for Cardiff when I was 14. It really was a dream come true. There were no feelings of nerves though; I was so excited to be a part of it all. Goose bumps and adrenaline were running through me and I couldn't wait to get my opportunity to play.

The club was only attracting around 4,000 fans to each game at the time but it was still the most people I had ever played in front of, so to me it felt like being in the Nou Camp. Anyway, 4,000 Cardiff City fans at Ninian Park will usually make more noise than 10,000 fans at most other clubs. The atmosphere at a Cardiff City game is usually special and the fans are passionate.

I started the game on the bench but after 20 minutes Chris Greenacre took a knock to his eye. Kenny told me to warm up so I rushed out of the dug out to have a jog along the touchline in front of the Grandstand. As I looked up into the director's box I saw my family smiling and waving at me, including Mum and Pops who were sat together despite their separation. It was a lovely feeling seeing them all so happy, in spite of their recent problems, and I was made up that I had been responsible for that.

As I was warming up, looking up at my parents in the stand, I could see out of the corner of my eye that Kenny was waving at me to get back to the dug out. I jogged back towards him thinking I was going to sit back down but then he told me, 'You're going on'. I couldn't believe that this was going to be it. At most I had been expecting a few minutes at the end of the game so to go on with the majority of the match still to be played was a dream.

Those first couple of steps running onto the pitch were unreal. The crowd must have known that I was a local boy making my debut as they gave me a loud cheer and that meant a lot to me. I had loads of excited energy bubbling inside me and spent the first couple of minutes tearing around trying to get involved.

The game went by in a blur but I remember feeling confident and not out of place. I also managed to set up the winning goal when a cross came in and I headed it back across the six-yard box for Jeff Eckhardt to tap the ball over the line.

We won the game 2–1 and unbelievably I was named man of the match on my debut. The day couldn't have gone much better. As I came off the pitch Joan Hill, the club's Chief Executive, gave me a hug. She was brilliant to me throughout her time at Cardiff and we became close. I was this rough and rugged kid from Llanrumney but she looked out for me and I will never forget that. Joan must have been in her forties at the time but all the players fancied her; she was a petite blonde and she wore tight black leather trousers, which used to get all the boys talking. Everyone loved her as she was such a genuine person and even after we both left Cardiff we kept in touch and exchanged Christmas presents.

After picking up a bottle of champagne for my man of the match performance, I had to catch the bus back home. So much for the glamour of life as a professional footballer! When I got back to the house all the family was waiting for me so we cracked open my bottle of champagne and had a little celebration. Everyone was so happy for me and it was a lovely moment in my life. I was going out with the boys that night and I remember that as I got changed I felt on top of the world.

First thing on Sunday morning I went straight out and bought almost every paper that was likely to have a match report of the game and spent hours dissecting every word. The *South Wales Echo* was particularly complimentary and said:

> The player who made the most impact was 17 year old Christian Roberts, a second year YTS trainee from Llanrumney. Roberts had found himself plunged into his Nationwide League debut as Chris Greenacre was taken to hospital after taking a severe bang to the head.
>
> Even Hibbitt was unsure how Roberts would react. He had never before played in front of more than a handful of spectators for City's youth team and suddenly he was running out at Ninian Park in front of 4,000 plus.
>
> And he loved it. He made the most of his experience, looking assured and settling in immediately. He missed a good chance, heading disastrously wide from a clear opening, but as he covered his face with his hands in horror, the fans applauded him warmly.
>
> Kenny Hibbitt said of the young star 'Christian did brilliant. We've been watching him develop for a while and he only did what we expected from him. He has great ability and great spring for a wee chap—it was a good debut'.

The article ended by saying that my 'contribution was immense' and I had enjoyed an 'outstanding debut'. I must have read that report a hundred times, I couldn't stop smiling and it boosted my confidence through the roof.

Going into training on the Monday I was buzzing and felt that I could definitely make a mark in the Football League. We had a game on Tuesday night against Chester so everyone was sharp and focussed, trying to earn their place in the squad, and I was hopeful that I would be involved. Training started well, and in a practice game I was flying, when all of a sudden disaster struck. I twisted awkwardly and my knee buckled which led me to collapse in agony on the floor. I didn't want to show that I was hurt so I tried to get straight back up but as I did I felt this searing rush of pain shoot through my knee and I immediately fell back down.

'Oi! Don't start messing around like you're a big time Charlie now. Put it in!' Russell shouted at me. I tried to get to my feet again but after a few steps I knew something was wrong. Russell lost his rag a bit; I think he thought I was putting it on, so he angrily ushered me away to see the physio. It turned out that I had again torn the cartilage in my knee and would need an operation. After everything had seemed to be going so well I was absolutely gutted as I had broken into the first team and now faced a few months on the sideline.

Yet there was a silver lining, as without suffering that injury I may not have ever met my future wife. On the Friday of the week I got injured I was feeling a bit down so my brother Matthew dragged me into town to stop me feeling so sorry for myself. We went to a club and I noticed a blonde woman start speaking to my mate Kevin. He came over and told me she had been asking about me. I was only 17 at the time, and she was clearly older than me, so I couldn't believe my luck.

She eventually walked over and introduced herself. Her name was Janine, she was 27, and had recently moved back to Cardiff after working for the Fraud Squad in London for a few years. When she told me she was 27, I panicked and instinctively told her that I was 22. She didn't have a clue about football and didn't know that I played for Cardiff, but she didn't seem interested anyway when I told her. We spent the rest of the night flirting away and hit it off immediately. At the end of the night we took each other's numbers and promised to meet up again soon.

The following week we went on our first date when we arranged to meet at TGI Fridays. I knew I would have to tell her the truth about my age but I wasn't sure how she would take it. In the end I just came out with it, 'Look,' I sheepishly said, 'I'm only 19'. She didn't seem too bothered so I decided to go for broke, 'Actually that's not true. I'm 17'. She froze, and for a moment I thought I had blown it, but we carried on with the date and despite the age difference it was obvious that we had a connection. Following that initial date we started to see each other regularly and began a relationship.

My rehab from my knee injury initially went well and I was starting to think I would soon be back challenging for a place in the first team when the knee went again in a reserve team match. I couldn't believe it; I would need another operation and more weeks of intense rehab. I was gutted but I never doubted that I would get back.

Whilst I was injured Russell Osman was sacked from his position as joint manager. The day he was told to leave I remember he literally left Ninian Park via the back door. He was too embarrassed to collect his boots and trainers from the dressing room himself so he asked me to fetch them for him. As he left he told me to look after myself and that was it, he was gone. I was sad to see him go, as after all, he had been partly responsible for giving me my debut in the first team but the dynamic of joint managers hadn't really worked and the team had struggled to pick up results.

In fact things didn't improve much under Kenny Hibbitt and he also finally made way. The club appointed Frank Burrows as the new manager, which unnerved me a bit as I was only a youngster with one professional game under my belt so I would have to prove myself all over again. Frank was a gruff Scot who had led Cardiff to promotion during his previous spell at the club during the 1980s and he had a good reputation in the game. I knew it was not going to be easy to convince him that I deserved a place in the first team and I was going to have to work my bollocks off.

My case wasn't helped when, nearing full fitness, I was involved in an incident that had me worried sick. One Saturday night I went into town with some friends and collapsed. An ambulance took me to hospital and it turned out that some idiot had spiked my drink with drugs. I can honestly say that whilst I may have got through an ocean of alcohol during my life that I have never touched drugs, as it is something that has never appealed to me. When I found out my drink had been spiked I was worried about how it would look to the new manager and I debated whether to tell Frank about it.

On the Monday morning I decided that honesty was the best policy so I went to see Frank and told him what had happened. I wasn't sure what he was going to say but I thought that he may have been sympathetic and put an arm around me, but he was furious. He told me in no uncertain terms, 'Sort out who you hang around with, and the places you go, otherwise I'll sack you'. I was shocked but it was good advice. I really wish I had taken it over the years.

After three months away from the game I finally made my comeback in a nice low-key game, the Welsh derby, against Swansea at the Vetch Field. The Welsh derby is a massive game, right up there with the fiercest derbies in British football. The fans despise each other and the atmosphere at the games is always intense.

It was no different that day at the Vetch, it was bubbling. I hated playing there, it was a real shit hole. I don't say that just because Swansea played there but because it was. It had four crappy little stands and the fans were right on top of you; it was like a bear pit.

I was on the bench that day and as I was warming up with our black striker, John Williams, a section of the Jacks gave him some shocking racial abuse. Typically, Willo brushed it aside and didn't answer back but I was raging for him, I almost felt like diving in the crowd and smacking the idiots chanting that filth. Ironically Willo had previously played for Swansea, and would return there after playing for Cardiff, where he would help them achieve promotion. I wonder if those who were abusing him ended up cheering him on?

Frank sent me on with only 20 minutes remaining and I remember sprinting to keep a ball from going out of play. As I ran for the ball I had to slow myself down as otherwise I was going to end up in the crowd and if I had done that then there was no way I would have emerged unscathed. The place was more or less on the right side of anarchy but it wouldn't have taken much to spark a riot. In the end the game finished 1–1 and I felt I had again done myself justice in trying circumstances.

Next we faced Doncaster Rovers at Ninian Park. I was in the starting line up for the first time and I fancied my chances of grabbing my first goal as Doncaster were really struggling.

The day went better than I could ever have imagined. We were all on fire and everything we hit went in as we absolutely battered Doncaster and ended up recording Cardiff's biggest win in over 40 years when we won 7–1. Having only been 2–0 up at halftime I helped us open the floodgates when the Doncaster keeper was sent off for a foul on me. Ironically, I had spent some time in Ibiza the previous summer with Doncaster's sub goalkeeper, Robert Pell, so that kicked off some banter.

Once they were down to 10 men we set about them and started to score with virtually every attack. My first goal in professional football came in front of the Canton Stand after 55 minutes. I was one on one with the keeper and opted to go around him but my touch was a bit heavy and that left me with a tight angle to squeeze the ball into the goal but somehow I wrapped my foot around the ball and it went in.

When the ball hit the net I went bonkers. I jumped on a fence to celebrate with the fans but managed to get my hands covered in anti vandalism paint. It was all over my shirt and everything. I certainly didn't envision celebrating my first goal in professional football covered in paint. The club even tried to charge me for the state of my shirt as it was covered in the stuff.

The next day I once again bought any newspaper that had a match report on the game and devoured every word. The *South Wales Echo* gave me a score of 9 out of 10, named me as man of the match, and said:

> Every Cardiff player was able to walk off yesterday secure in the knowledge that they had strengthened their chances of staying at Ninian Park next season under Burrows' new regime. But a few stood out above the rest. Teenage striker Roberts, aged 18, was given his first start in the senior team and acquitted himself superbly.
>
> 'He was lively and apart from scoring he made some good runs', said Ayre. 'Away from matches he has a good attention span and takes in what he is told, that can be unusual for young players. He can be pleased with his performance and I had a quiet word with him when he was replaced by Steve White. That was no reflection on Christian—we wanted to give him his own personal moment of applause from the spectators. He deserved it.'

It's fair to say that I was well chuffed with myself. In my first three appearances the team hadn't lost and now I was off the mark as well. I was beginning to consider myself as some sort of lucky charm and I think the fans did too as they took to me.

Next up was a long trip up to Hull and I scored my

first away goal to give the team a 1–0 win. It was a great feeling scoring my first away goal as the fans who travel away are generally hardcore and they went nuts when the ball went in.

By this stage I felt like a proper first team player as I was playing regularly, scoring goals and had signed my first professional contract. Getting a decent deal from the club was a hassle though. I wasn't happy with the first offer the club made so I decided to ask the PFA to give me a hand with negotiating. They tried to get me a ridiculous deal, which frankly the club was never going to give me. In the end Frank made it clear that all the club could afford was £225.00 a week, £50.00 an appearance and £50.00 a goal. He also offered me a £3,000 signing on fee. It was a pretty crap deal but I wanted to sign the contract and officially call myself a professional footballer.

The rest of the season went pretty well for me even though I only scored one more goal in a 2–1 defeat to Macclesfield at Ninian Park. The team had struggled over the course of the season but seemed to pick up once Frank had taken charge, even though we still only just avoided relegation. There seemed to be a real belief amongst the squad that the following season could be one where we would regroup and become promotion contenders. I was confident that I would be a key part of that team.

5

GOING DOWNHILL

That summer I really knuckled down and worked hard on my fitness in an effort to make the most of my opportunity at Cardiff. I was absolutely determined to do whatever was required in order to cement my place as a first team player. There were definitely no Ibiza trips, or heavy drinking sessions, I ate properly and trained regularly by myself.

Shortly before pre-season kicked off I remember the phone went in the house. I was upstairs at the time so Pops took the call. The voice on the other end of the line said to him, 'Is Christian there please? It's Frank Burrows from Cardiff City'.

Pops put the receiver down on the table and screamed up the stairs 'Chris! Phone for you!'

Unfortunately, he didn't tell me who it was so I ran down the stairs, thinking it was one of my mates, and when I picked up the phone I casually said, 'Yo yo yo, who's this?'

A gruff Scottish accent answered, 'Chris. It's Frank Burrows'. My heart sank, I must have sounded like a right idiot. 'I want to meet you on Monday morning in my office,' Frank said.

'Shit! He's going to let me go!' I pessimistically

assumed.

Thankfully Frank wanted to see me to discuss an improved contract. He offered me a three-year deal with more money and to use a famous football cliché, I was over the moon. Frank told me to keep working hard and if I did I could become an established player at Cardiff. I was desperate to prove him right and I was geared up to work my nuts off that pre-season.

Strangely, however, when I reported for duty I felt far from being a first team player, if anything I felt ousted. Frank gave me squad number 23 out of 24 and I thought that was a bit naughty. It wasn't as if I expected to be 9 or 10 but by being given 23 it was clear I was way down the pecking order. This was before the days when first team players had all sorts of numbers, generally if you weren't given a number from 2 to 11 then you wouldn't be starting. The whole attitude towards me seemed to be a bit dismissive as well. I didn't have a clue what was going on so I didn't go into that season in the best frame of mind.

After Frank offered me a new contract I thought he saw me as a first time squad player so I was bewildered to find that I wasn't in his plans at all. I was never told why I wasn't featuring and that made me unbelievably frustrated. Every now and then I would get a few minutes on the pitch but what was I supposed to do in that time? The team were near the top of the table so Frank obviously didn't want to break up a winning team. That meant I spent more time kicking my heels in the reserves.

My objective of getting into the first team wasn't helped by the emergence of Robert Earnshaw. Earnie was a year younger than me but it was obvious that

Frank had taken a shine to him. As we were both so young we were never included in a squad together, unless there was an injury crisis. It was immediately apparent that it would be a straight fight between Earnie and me for an opportunity to play.

In all honesty I didn't see why Earnie and me had to compete with each other, as we were very different players. Earnie was a poacher who worked on the shoulder of the defenders and waited for his chance. When the ball finally came his way in the penalty area it invariably ended up in the back of the net. In comparison I used to play deeper than Earnie and liked to be involved in the build up play. My Dad drummed into me as a kid that whilst scoring a goal was nice I should get pleasure out of setting goals up as well and that motto became a habit. It meant that I didn't score as many goals as Earnie but I would get on the ball more and despite what Frank felt, I was confident that we could have played together.

For the first game of the season I was left out of the squad that travelled to Hartlepool, but Earnie was included. My mood wasn't improved when I heard that Cardiff won 1–0 and Earnie had scored the winner on his debut. It wasn't any old goal either, it was an absolute world-class bicycle kick and when I saw it I thought, 'Cheers Earn. That hasn't done me any favours'. Obviously I was happy for Earnie, as he's a cracking lad and has proven over the years that he's a quality player, but at the time I was a youngster eager to play and it was clear that the manager already had him pencilled in ahead of me before that ridiculous goal.

At this point I was still seeing Janine and we decided

to buy a two-bedroom house in a new housing estate called Pontprennau in Cardiff. Not long after moving in together, Janine seemed to be feeling a bit ill so I went out and bought her a puppy to cheer her up. She loved it but she said she had something to tell me . . . she was pregnant.

I had recently turned 18 and the news took me back a bit. I told her that it would be stupid to have the baby as I was so young and we hadn't been together for long. Janine agreed and she booked herself in for an abortion. It was a tough time, and I wasn't sure whether I was coming or going, but then the night before she was scheduled to go into hospital I realised that I wanted us to have the baby. We talked about it throughout the night and in the end we were both relieved that she wasn't going through with it. For some reason it felt right that we should have this baby together. We were happy and started making plans for a future when we would have a little one join us.

Then sometime in January 1999, in the middle of the night, Janine went to the toilet. I was only half awake when I heard a piercing scream. Her waters had broken and she was only a few months into the pregnancy. We knew that it wasn't a good sign.

Without hesitating we rushed into the hospital and at first the situation seemed under control. The doctor initially seemed positive, and I began to relax, but then he came out to find me with a serious look on his face. He explained to me that we had lost the baby. I was numb. I don't think I cried or said anything, I didn't know what to do with myself.

The baby had died whilst still inside Janine and she had to give birth knowing that, unlike after most births, she wouldn't hear the cry of our first child just a deathly silence. It seems too horrible to think about, even now. We named our daughter Olivia and whilst she wasn't in this world long we loved her dearly.

Unbelievably, despite this tragedy, I still went into work the next day. Looking back I was probably in shock and not thinking properly. I told Frank Burrows what had happened and he was brilliant. The club didn't have much money back then but he arranged for us to go to Tenerife for a week to get away from everything. I really appreciated it as I thought it would do Janine some good.

To be honest I wasn't too bad when I was out in Tenerife. What had happened still hadn't really hit me but Janine was distraught. Whilst we were away my Mum organised Olivia's funeral, which took a huge burden off us, so we could concentrate on getting our heads together.

When we returned we had to go to the funeral and that's when it all hit me like a sledgehammer. Seeing Olivia's tiny white coffin killed me, and everything that I had kept inside over the last week came flooding out. I was in pieces. My little girl should have had her whole life in front of her but it was stopped in its tracks before she took her first breath. I couldn't believe what had happened. It all seemed like a nightmare and I was devastated.

Janine and I were both desperate to have a baby together so we started trying for another child straight away. Within weeks Janine announced that she was pregnant and it seemed like the very least that we deserved after what we had been through.

In spite of that good news I was still struggling to

come to terms with everything, and unsurprisingly I wasn't playing much for Cardiff. Frank Burrows thought it may do me some good to get some games for Drogheda in the Irish League. Cardiff had a link with Drogheda as the club's former manager, Eddie May, was in charge there. The plan was that I would train with Cardiff all week and then fly to Dublin every Friday morning. I would play for Drogheda on the Saturday and then be back in Cardiff on the Monday.

It sounded great at first, as I could look after Janine whilst she was pregnant, and still play some football. In principle it was a good idea but it didn't quite work out like that, even though my time in Ireland did do me some good.

Drogheda wasn't too far from Dublin so if I'm honest all I did in Ireland was go out on the piss. I was struggling to get over Olivia and my time out there allowed me to blow off some steam away from Cardiff.

The first few games for Drogheda actually went well as I scored a few goals, and put in some good performances, but the standard of football was poor and I quickly lost interest. It was so bad that I began to think I didn't need to prepare properly and started to drink on the Friday night before games.

My drinking wasn't too bad until Cardiff sent Dai Thomas to join me in Ireland and then it went into overdrive. Dai joined Cardiff for big money from Watford and he was expected to be one of the club's top players but he was carrying a bit of weight and liked his food and drink, which meant he was never at his best. Frank used to go crazy and scream at him to slim down but he really wasn't interested. It was a shame as Dai was a talented footballer. He could have been a special player at that level but he didn't want it.

Dai was a crazy and funny guy though and made for great company. He was as hard as nails as well, big, broad and solidly built and he knew a few dodgy characters around South Wales. Despite all that he was a wicked guy and he used to have me in stitches. We had some great banter between us and I enjoyed having him in Ireland with me, even if we did both go off the rails.

Our weekends together turned into a 48 hour party. On the Friday night, before games, we hit it hard and didn't care that we were meant to be playing the next day. On Dai's first Friday in Drogheda we went a bit mental and he was so ill the next day that he didn't turn up for the game.

Drogheda could have been a very nice opportunity football wise but I didn't take it. Nearly the whole time I was there I was either drunk or hungover. I used to call Eddie May and tell him that I was too ill or injured to play and I think he gave up on me in the end. On the football front it wasn't the best but those few weeks I had at Drogheda certainly let me get stuff off my chest, which is what I desperately needed.

Looking back now there are probably better ways to sort out your issues rather than drink. I should have gone to counselling but I was only 18 and didn't know any better. I didn't talk to anyone about my problems, I let them all fester inside me and even though my time in Ireland made me feel a bit better I never fully resolved those issues. They buried themselves deep inside me and would then erupt later on in my career.

After about six weeks I told Frank that I had enough at Drogheda and was ready to knuckle down at Cardiff and fight for my place again. I had no intention of pissing my career away and had treated the time at Drogheda as a holiday. With a relatively clear mind, and renewed hunger, I was ready to work hard and break into the team, if I got the opportunity.

But then disaster struck again, Janine had a miscarriage. We had lost two babies in the space of six months. It was a terrible time and the two of us were horrendously upset. 'Why is this happening to us?' we kept asking ourselves.

Matters weren't helped by my inability to get anywhere near the first team. Cardiff were flying at this stage of the season and were looking set to win promotion to the third tier of the English football pyramid. No matter how hard I tried, or how well I played in the reserves, I couldn't get a chance to show what I was capable of. Frank could tell that I was frustrated, and he was keen for me to get some games, so he decided to send me to Hereford on loan for two months.

Hereford were playing in the Conference at this time and I was irritated as I had to commute every day to train. I suppose my attitude wasn't the best as I was still reeling from what Janine and I had been through. Being out of the picture at Cardiff also left me angry and bitter. It was a dark stage of my life and being at Hereford didn't pick me up. I didn't respectfully think that this was an opportunity to play and prove myself. I felt it was all a bit shit and I let the situation drag me down. The ground was crap, the training facilities were poor and the standard of football was shocking. It was demoralising and I couldn't wait to get away from the place.

I certainly didn't feel like a professional footballer at Hereford. I remember for one away game we had to leave at six in the morning so I had to stay in digs in Hereford the night before. As a first team player I didn't think that was a good way to prepare and as a result my own standards dropped.

To be honest I was glad when that season ended. For the club it had been a tremendous season, as we had gained automatic promotion, but it had all been a bit of a disaster on a professional and personal level for me. I should have looked forward to playing at a higher level but by the time pre-season came around I still hadn't pulled myself together. My confidence had taken a knock and it was clear that my face didn't fit at the club.

During pre-season I was sulking a bit and that showed in my performances, which were lacklustre to say the least. I was desperate for someone to take an interest in me, to give me some encouragement but no one seemed bothered. Some extra coaching on finishing and movement would have lifted me, in fact any sort of interest in me whatsoever would have helped but I felt used and abused. I was only 19 but I was already beginning to feel as if I had been consigned to the scrap heap. The level of disrespect grew so great towards me that all I got in training was being sent on five-mile runs around Cardiff. I felt embarrassed, furious and fed up.

Every time I did get a sniff in the first team I felt under huge pressure to do something and impress. If I didn't score I felt that the management was happy to put another nail into my coffin. By this stage I had developed an attitude and I have no doubt now that it didn't do me any favours. I constantly thought, 'Fuck them', and it showed.

After all the build up, scrapping away to make it as a pro, emerging on the scene like a bright spark, everything seemed to drop dead for me. I never thought I would have ever wanted to leave Cardiff but I was desperate to get away to somewhere I would be appreciated. My faith in my ability never wavered and I was sure that with a fresh start I could prove those who doubted me at Cardiff wrong.

Over the previous two seasons I had made only 21 appearances in the first team and hadn't scored a single goal. I knew that if I was given a run in the team I could score goals but I didn't have the same chances that Earnie had. The team did poorly in the Third Division and were relegated that season back to the bottom division but still no one gave me an opportunity.

I was a nightmare at home, constantly moody and depressed. All the good things that I had going for me, such as having a supportive girlfriend, a nice house and playing professional football for my hometown team, never occurred to me. I focussed on all the negatives in my life and I think Janine must have found it hard to deal with me at times. Those two years were tough. I was cast into the wilderness.

I can't recall many games that I played for Cardiff over that period in my life but the one that comes to mind was an away game at Millwall. Cardiff and Millwall games always provide a feisty atmosphere, and usually mean trouble. This game was no different. I remember Dai Thomas and me standing on top of the toilets after the game looking outside to see Cardiff and Millwall fans battering each other. Watching all these guys going at it didn't seem real and it was ironic that within a year Dai would himself get caught up in hooligan activities when he was arrested at Euro 2000.

I spent most of that campaign rotting away in the reserves. We weren't in a proper reserve league so we had to make the most of games that we did have. The games against Exeter, home and away, soon resulted in an upturn in my fortunes.

Even though I had a year left on my contract it was obvious that the club didn't want me around so I knew that I had to start scrapping for my career as a professional footballer to earn a chance to move on to another league club. When we played Exeter, at St James Park, I played out of my skin and scored an absolute screamer. After the return fixture at Ninian Park, Exeter's reserve team manager, John Cornforth, came up to me and said 'What's going on with you here then?'

'To be honest John I think my time is up. I'm looking for a new challenge now,' I replied.

We left it at that and I didn't think anything of it but that conversation soon had huge ramifications on my career.

6

A FRESH START

The summer of 2000 marked a fresh start in my personal and professional life. Janine had told me that she was pregnant again earlier in the year, and although we were both apprehensive after everything we had been through, this time things finally worked out for us. Despite another close call, she gave birth to Ethan William Ian Roberts on 5 June 2000.

We had been through hell together so it was unbelievably special to be able to welcome our little baby boy into the world. For the first few weeks we couldn't take our eyes off him, certain that something would go wrong. I carried Ethan everywhere with me and I was the proudest father around.

Frank Burrows had left Cardiff following the team's relegation and you would have thought I was looking forward to a new start. Unfortunately his coach, Billy Ayre, took over and things went from bad to worse. Billy literally showed no interest in me whatsoever. One day that summer Billy called me into his office and told me I wasn't going to feature over the final year of my contract and that he would let me speak to other clubs. He then dropped the bombshell that he had already sorted out talks for me at Barry Town and Merthyr

Tydfil; a Welsh league team and a non-league team. My blood was boiling and I made it clear to him that I was confident I could do a job in the Football League and that I would not be dropping out of it. He almost seemed dismissive of my ambition and it was obvious he thought I couldn't cut it as a League player.

Out of courtesy I went to see a representative of Barry Town, who were the top Welsh Premier club at the time, but I had no intention of signing for them. I was offered a brown paper bag full of cash to play in their Champions League qualifier games but I wasn't interested.

After I told Billy that under no circumstances would I be moving to a non-league club, he made that summer hell for me. I wasn't included in the first team squad photo, or given a squad number, despite still having a year of my contract left. Two years previously I was a hot prospect but now I was being discarded without a second thought. I was devastated and I didn't think I deserved to be treated so poorly.

Thankfully, John Cornforth at Exeter hadn't forgotten about me and he called to see if I was interested in a move there. I jumped at the chance and told him that if we could agree terms then I would love to play for Exeter City. They were a small club, but still in the Football League, and I felt I could make my mark up there. It was also a nice feeling to be wanted after being made to feel like a spare part for so long.

Thinking about my new life at Exeter really psyched me up, so imagine my disappointment when Billy Ayre refused to let me speak to them. The first team was on tour in Ireland at the time and I was left wasting away at home with the YTS boys. When I found this out I went ballistic. He wanted me out but I couldn't understand why he wouldn't let me speak to Exeter. Billy may have passed away now, and maybe it's not the done thing to say it, but I certainly hated him at the time for the way he treated me.

Having just had a baby boy I was determined to provide for him and Janine, yet this man wanted to heap more misery on us. There was no way I was standing for it, my emotions boiled over and without hesitating I rang Billy and let him have it. I told him that if he didn't let me go to Exeter I would see out the rest of my contract at Cardiff and he would effectively be paying me to sit on my backside. He didn't like that but I had him by the balls so he reluctantly let me talk to Exeter. It hurt me that it had come to this because Cardiff were my team but I had no choice, it was either play hard ball or watch my career go down the toilet.

My agent, Mel Stein, accompanied me to Exeter for talks and we were both confident that we could reach an agreement. Mel was my first agent, and he had been Gazza's representative for most of his career, so I assumed I was in good hands. At Exeter we quickly agreed a deal and whilst it was all being typed up I went out to train at the club's Cat and Fiddle training ground and Mel shot off.

When the contract was ready to be signed, I returned to the office to put pen to paper. Thankfully, before signing, I quickly re-read it again only to find that Exeter had changed the deal. They had shaved money off my basic salary, appearance and goal bonuses. I couldn't believe it. I was getting screwed again!

I stormed out and got in the car to drive back to

Cardiff. My head was all over the place, what did I have to do to get a break in this game? On the way back I rang Mel and told him what had happened and he couldn't believe it. It makes you wonder how many players have been screwed over the years by clubs changing contracts at the last minute.

To rub salt into the wound, Exeter started putting it about in the local press that I was some kind of prima donna who was after more money. That wound me up as I was simply a kid trying to play football, and provide for his family, and it seemed as if everyone wanted to ruin my life.

The deal looked to be dead in the water, and I was facing up to the prospect of another morale-shredding year at Cardiff, when Blakey rang me out of the blue and tried to make amends. 'Look Chris. I apologise,' he said, eating plenty of humble pie, 'let's start over again. We have a bunch of friendly games coming up and I want you involved. The contract we initially agreed is still on the table.'

I wasn't happy to be messed around but it was an opportunity to continue to play in the Football League so I went back up the M5 and signed a two-year contract for £450.00 a week. For a footballer the money was a bit crap but I didn't care, this was a chance to prove myself.

It's funny but I remember thinking, even before I had made my debut for Exeter, that under no circumstances would I extend my two-year contract. I was ready to play my heart out for the club, and prove I was a good player, but I was confident that within those two years I could make bigger clubs take notice of me and earn a move. I was going to do everything possible to better myself in that time; I was a man on a mission. No more feeling sorry for myself or sulking, this was going to be it!

Arrogance was a big part of my make up back then but I think that gave me the ingrained belief that I could make it where others may have chosen to drop out of the League. At this time my arrogance was channelled in the right direction and it paid dividends for me as it propelled me forwards. Within a few years I would be consumed by my own self-importance and it had a detrimental effect on my life and career.

The first year at Exeter was hard because I lived in Devon whilst Janine stayed in Cardiff with Ethan. It was tough having to leave my baby boy behind but Janine and I decided that for me to progress I initially needed to be close to the club to concentrate on my football.

For the first couple of weeks I was put up in a huge house, with the other new signings, until I found a place to live. That summer at Exeter was mental. The club released 12 players and brought in 15, all on free transfers. There seemed to be a new player coming to live in that house every day. Most of the lads had been jettisoned by their previous clubs, like me, so we were all now looking for a chance to prove people wrong. I suppose we were a rag tag group of guys eager to make a point.

In the house Blakey stayed downstairs, so he could keep an eye on all of us, but at night that didn't stop Andy Roscoe, Graham Tomlinson and me from jumping out of the second floor window so we could go to the pub. We never went stupid; we were all young lads looking to escape the boredom of staying in and it allowed us to get to know each other a little better.

When I saw Exeter's fixtures for the new season I couldn't believe it, our first game was against Cardiff at St James Park. A few weeks after leaving Cardiff City I would be making my debut against my old club. Even though I had only been away from the club for a few weeks, Cardiff City had changed beyond all recognition from the club that I had known. The old Wimbledon chairman, Sam Hammam, had purchased Cardiff and embarked on a huge spending spree, which saw him bring in the likes of Danny Gabbidon and Rhys Weston for big money. Ex-Wales boss, Bobby Gould had also been appointed as manager so I did start to wonder what may have happened if I had sat tight for a few more weeks.

Billy Ayre remained at the club as he was Gould's assistant, and I was still seething with injustice over how he had treated me. I was looking forward to settling some scores with him when I faced my old club. That thought fired me up and I busted a gut in training to ensure that I was as fit and sharp as possible for my day of redemption.

Yet a few days before the game Blakey pulled me to one side and informed me, 'After everything that has gone on at Cardiff I think it's best you start on the bench on Saturday'.

My first thought was, 'What a twat!' But despite being gutted, I got on with it and was confident that I would get my chance. Looking back now I can see why he left me out, as it must have been obvious that I was still raw and liable to get myself sent off.

The big match arrived on a hot August day; perfect for football, and I was distraught that I wasn't starting.

It was strange seeing my old mates at Cardiff in the warm up, whilst I was with another team, but it wasn't a day to reminisce, it was a day to get even. Billy tried to shake my hand before the game but I refused. There was no way I was shaking his hand, I had to restrain myself from punching him if anything.

With about 20 minutes to go we were losing 2–1 and Blakey finally threw me on. I was so wound up I wasn't even thinking about the football, I was full of venom and vengeance. Within 30 seconds of entering the fray I kicked Cardiff's full-back, Matty Brazier, right up in the air. It caused a huge fight and earned me a ticking off by the ref and a bollocking by Blakey. He was pointing at his temple screaming 'Use your fucking head you idiot!' I didn't have a head by this point, I was a loose cannon. In my mind I was booting Billy Ayre. Seeing Matty sprawled on the floor brought me to my senses and I apologised to him. He knew that I had lost my head, and I think he appreciated my circumstances, so he was cool about it.

We ended up losing the game 2–1 and whilst I was disappointed I knew that over the course of that season my time would come. Despite Cardiff winning that game Billy didn't last long at Cardiff as within a few weeks he was out and I have to admit I was happy that he had failed. At one point I heard that Sam Hammam and Bobby Gould were looking at ways to take me back to Cardiff, and whilst I was flattered, I concentrated on making a name for myself at Exeter.

During those first six weeks at Exeter I probably played some of the best football of my career, even though the team had a terrible start. We actually didn't win until our eighth game of the season and we found ourselves near the bottom of the league.

I had managed to break my goal scoring duck in our fourth match, against Hartlepool; where we drew 1–1. It was my first goal in 26 games and after two years in the wilderness, and getting treated like shit, I felt a huge surge of adrenalin and relief when that ball hit the net.

It felt so good to be wanted again and my confidence gradually began to return which served to improve my performances. At times I felt a bit like a big fish in a small pond, after coming from a relatively large club like Cardiff, to what was almost a small village club like Exeter, but I flourished in that environment.

St James Park may have been small, and the facilities were basic, but I felt at home. The fans always cheered me on and everyone around the place radiated warmth. My Dad and Janine also enjoyed coming to watch me play as all the staff treated them so well.

As a place to live it was fantastic as well. Exeter is an attractive, historic city with beautiful countryside and seaside resorts surrounding it. I loved everything about the place and certainly didn't regret my move down to Devon. At that time in my career Exeter was the perfect place for me to play; they knew I was like a wounded animal so they wrapped me up in cotton wool and helped put me together again.

Having a manager who believed in me played a key part in my career revival but I had a love-hate relationship with Noel Blake. Blakey knew how to get the best out of me, as some games he showered me with praise and said, 'Go out and express yourself,' but if he felt I wasn't pulling my weight he screamed in my face.

Blakey was a massive black bloke; with arms like bazookas and when he lost it he really went to town. In a game against Mansfield, I hadn't had the best first half, and he was doing his nut at half time. I thought he was going over the top so I piped up to say something and he went for me. He was right in my face, his eyes popping out of his head, screaming, whilst showering me with his spit, 'If you don't sort your fucking attitude out you little dick then me and you are going to have it after the game. Don't bother coming back in if you don't put some fucking effort in'.

Some players don't respond to that sort of treatment but I was brought up in a similar environment so it was normal for me. My Mum and Dad weren't ones to ask me to do things softly and nicely, they always shouted at me and to be honest that's what I responded to. In the second half against Mansfield I played out of my skin and helped us to a 1–0 win. Thankfully Blakey must have appreciated my second half efforts, as he was all smiles after the game.

The only drawback during my time at Exeter was the away trips. As we were so far down south any games in the north of the country, against teams such as Carlisle and Darlington, resulted in a nightmare journey on the team coach. We didn't have the money to fly to games so we spent hours on the coach going up and down motorways. After travelling all day we had the pleasure of staying in bed and breakfasts that made Fawlty Towers look like a five star establishment. Some of the places that we stayed in were horrific but we understood that the club was on a budget so we never complained. If anything staying in shit holes brought us closer together and we had a good laugh about it.

No egos at Exeter City were too big for a basic B&B.

A few weeks into the season I finally found a place to live with my teammate, Andy Burrows, in the Quay area of the city. It was a proper bachelor pad, I swear all we had in there were two settees, a TV and a bed in each room. It was like *Men Behaving Badly* in that flat, it was a right state at times.

At Exeter we usually had Wednesdays off, and on those occasions when I didn't go back to Cardiff to see Janine and Ethan, I would go on an all dayer with Graham Tomlinson and some of the lads.

We usually started at a pub at around midday, had some food, a gin and tonic and read the papers. By mid afternoon we would pick up the pace a bit, hit the fruit machines and up the drinking. Later on in the night, when we were steaming, we would do a bit of a pub crawl and end up in some dive nightclub. On some occasions we would invite most of the nightclub back to my flat down the Quay and we would be up all-night partying. After six months of these antics the landlord wrote a letter to the club to complain about our 'anti-social behaviour' and he kicked us out so we had to find new digs.

Of course I missed Janine and Ethan whilst I was living in Exeter but I was a young guy living away from home for the first time and making the most of my freedom. I almost needed that time on my own to grow up a bit and become my own person. On a personal level that first year at Exeter was fantastic and I feel that the stats don't really do me justice. I managed to get seven goals that year, which was a fair return, but my all round performance level was high and I worked my nuts off. Unfortunately the team didn't fare too well and we spent most of that season fighting relegation.

I suppose you can tell how much fun I had at Exeter by the state of some of my haircuts. For almost every game I had a different hairstyle and I must have bleached my hair every single colour going. The hairstyle the lads gave me the most stick over was when I had swirling lines razored in all the way over my head and through my beard, I looked nuts! My red mohawk also earned me a lot of abuse as well, particularly because none of the lads had actually seen it before I took to the field. During the warm up, and in the changing room, I wore a hat to hide it so as the game got underway it was the first time that everyone had seen it. Players from the opposition, and even my own teammates, caned me. Blakey and the lads used to shred me all the time but it was all good-natured and in the end they gave up.

During that first year my performances were so good at Exeter that they even earned me a call up into a few Wales Under 21 squads. My involvement with Wales had been non-existent over the years, despite having had a good reputation as a youngster. In order to get a game for the Under 21s, let alone the seniors, I was competing with the likes of Craig Bellamy, Robert Earnshaw, Simon Howarth, Leon Jeanne and Chris Llewellyn so it was tough but I was well chuffed when I got the call.

One of the great things about being called up was that I got to mix with the senior squad players, such as Ryan Giggs. There was me, scrapping away with Exeter City in the bottom division, rubbing shoulders with one of the game's greats. I remember spending some time watching the seniors train and the standard was unreal.

Players like Gary Speed and Mark Pembridge were top notch but Giggs was another level above, the things he was doing with a ball in training blew my mind.

Even though I was proud to be called up I never really felt part of the team, as I knew that when certain players returned to fitness they would replace me in the squad. It was great to represent my country, and get my caps, but in all honesty my international career wasn't anything to write home about. Still it was nice to gain some recognition. As I said earlier I especially enjoyed playing against Belarus where Leon Jeanne and me were in the starting line up. What are the odds of two best mates from childhood representing their country together?

Dad always told me that club comes before country, as clubs pay wages, and I strongly believed that. Exeter were the ones who provided me with the money to be able to afford food and shelter for my family so my priority was always towards them. I am as patriotic as most people but when you have a young son to provide for then he has to come above anything else.

My second season at Exeter was again productive and the fans appreciated my committed approach. That season I got booked 12 times and I received the first and only sending off in my career after two yellow cards against Rushden and Diamonds. I had a raging fire burning inside me after my experience at Cardiff, and sometimes it bubbled over. Yet that desire, coupled with my arrogance, made me a better player. I was determined to prove to everyone that I could be a force to be reckoned with in the Football League, despite what Billy Ayre thought of me.

I managed to get on the score sheet 11 times that

season, and in a game at Scunthorpe, I scored two of the best goals of my career. For the first goal I picked up the ball midway in the Scunthorpe half with my back to goal. As I received the ball I quickly turned, swivelled past my marker and set off towards the penalty area. When their centre back ran to tackle me I put the ball through his legs and then bent the ball into the corner of the net. The Scunny fans had been abusing me all game so as I ran off to celebrate I put my finger to my lips to silence the crowd.

With the fans' boos still ringing around the stadium I grabbed my second, which really shut them up. The ball came to me on the left hand side of the pitch, I ran inside, jinked past a defender and fired a shot from 25 yards into the bottom left hand corner. Ladies and gentlemen of Scunthorpe, I gave you Christian Roberts at his best and how did you respond? You pelted me with cigarette lighters!

Those goals are on You Tube and they probably sum me up as a player. I admit that I was a luxury player and when I was on song the fans were in for a treat but if I couldn't get my game going then I would be rubbish and the coach may as well take me off. The fans always seemed to forgive my bad games because they knew at that level I could do things with the ball that most others couldn't, so they rarely got on my back. The managers would have seizures due to my inability to play consistently and some of them gave me a right rollicking.

The second year at Exeter was a little harder for me on a personal level as I decided to move back to Cardiff due to missing my family so much. That year in Exeter had allowed me to grow up but I really felt I was missing out on Ethan's most important years and was desperate to be a good Dad. The only drawback to being at home was the daily commute to Exeter from Cardiff. It used to drive me crazy but Burger King in the services of J21–22 on the M5 did a roaring trade as almost every day, after training, I was so hungry I treated myself to a large bacon double cheeseburger meal. If I felt guilty about eating junk I wouldn't order the fries and convince myself that it was the healthy option!

Two months into my second season we were near the bottom of the league and as a result Noel Blake was sacked. I was obviously disappointed as Blakey had brought me to the club, and had believed in me, but I was happy when I found out that John Cornforth would be his successor.

As soon as Corny got the job he began badgering me to sign a contract extension. He kept reminding me that I owed him a favour due to him rescuing me from my hell at Cardiff. Every week he offered me a new contract but it was funny because it was always the same money but different ways of paying it. Whilst I did owe Corny a favour I stuck to my guns, I had promised I would stay for two years at Exeter and I intended to do that. Corny begged me to stay for one more year but after the years in the wilderness at Cardiff I still felt that I had some catching up to do and wanted to play at a higher level as soon as possible. By this stage I had also heard rumours that clubs such as Mansfield and Luton were sniffing around and I wanted to see who would come in for me once I became a free agent.

In the end I got so fed up with all of the speculation that I stupidly came out publicly and said to the press that no matter what happened I would not be signing a new contract at Exeter City. Understandably that upset a few of the fans and as soon as I said it I regretted it. Those people had been so good to me and I really didn't want to let them down. I had this desperation to play at a higher level as soon as possible and at the time all Exeter were aiming to do was survive in the old Division Three.

Thankfully, my hopes and prayers were soon answered. Over the course of the season I developed a groin problem, which kept flaring up. I told Corny that I would try to play through it but training every day seemed to aggravate it. As a result Corny gave me a few extra rest days a week, which I was grateful for, as not only did it help with the injury but I also got to stay at home with Ethan for a bit longer.

On one of those rest days I was driving up Rumney Hill in Cardiff (ironically this is exactly where I was when I told my Dad I wanted to sign for Cardiff) when my phone rang. It was Corny. He casually told me, 'We've had two offers for you today, one from Gillingham and one from Bristol City'. As soon as he said Bristol City I knew that was where I wanted to go. Bristol were a big club with strong support, a nice ground and a reputation for playing good football. They were also fighting for promotion to what we now call the Championship and were close to my Cardiff base. It was the perfect move for me on every level.

Corny told me not to get my hopes up just yet as there was still a lot of negotiating to be done but he would keep me informed of any developments. When

I put the phone down I was so excited. My plan of working hard for two years at Exeter to earn a move to a bigger club looked like it was going to pay off.

Within 10 minutes Corny rang me back with an update, 'We've accepted £100,000 offers from both clubs. Who do you want to talk to first?'

Without hesitating I said, 'Bristol City', and the wheels were then set in motion for me to complete a dream move to a big club in a higher division.

Making my debut for Cardiff City against Rochdale

Just about to score my first goal in the football league for Cardiff City against Doncaster Rovers

In action as a clean faced youngster for Cardiff City against Brighton

Cardiff City Youth Team, I'm in the middle row, third from left, Nathan 'Shaper' Cadette (middle row, second right), coach Gwynn Williams (back row, second from left)

Nice easy game to ease my way back from injury, the Welsh derby at The Vetch

Low key debut for Exeter City, against my old club Cardiff   © Jed Leicester/Press Association Images

The highlight of my career, scoring the last gasp winner for Bristol against Hartlepool in the play off semi final   © David Davies/Press Association Images

So close yet so far, almost scoring for Bristol against Brighton in the League One play off Final

© Nigel French/Press Association Images

Tussling with Alan Stubbs in a Carling Cup game for Bristol against Everton

© David Davies/Press Association Images

A rare sight, me putting in a tackle whilst in action for Swindon Town

Janine and Ethan

7

MOVING UP IN THE WORLD

By the time that Bristol City had expressed an interest in me, Mel Stein was no longer my agent. I found Mel hard work, to be honest, and I didn't think I was high on his list of priorities. I decided to join up with an agency called First Artists where John and Phil Smith, along with Alex Levac, looked after me. Alex actually became a good friend over time and we had a good working relationship.

Alex accompanied me to Bristol where we met the manager, Danny Wilson, at Ashton Gate for talks. By just walking into the ground I knew that this was a level above what I had been used to. In the club car park I parked my Peugeot 206 next to Mercedes, BMWs and other top cars and I thought, 'This is it! This is the big time!'

After feeling so comfortable at Exeter, and having managers who believed in me, it was important that I had a similar feeling at Bristol. Thankfully I immediately took to Danny Wilson. Not only was he a nice guy but he also had a good vision of where he wanted the club to go and I liked his philosophy on football. Danny believed in playing the ball on the ground, which suited my playing style and he saw me playing as a forward, rather than as a winger, which was my favourite position.

When Danny had finished selling the club to me I was more than happy to sign. So, whilst Alex negotiated my package with the chairman, I went off to do a medical, which I sailed through. When I returned Alex told me that they had offered me £800.00 a week, which was almost double the money that I was on at Exeter. However, I felt that I was worth more so I told Alex, 'Get it up to a £1,000.00 a week and I'll sign'.

It may have seemed like a mad move but I had an idea what the other players were earning at Bristol and I knew that even at £1,000.00 a week they were getting me cheap. Besides, I had worked so hard to get to this point that I wasn't going to be short changed now. Alex went back in with the chairman and not long afterwards he came out smiling. He had secured me £1,000.00 a week, £250.00 appearance bonus, £250.00 a goal and a £5,000.00 signing on fee. It wasn't quite the crazy money everyone assumes footballers earn but it was my first decent football contract and I finally felt that I had arrived.

At the time I was still living in the two bedroom house in Cardiff that Janine and I had bought shortly after I had signed my first professional contract. Across the road from us they were building some fantastic four bedroom houses which we had our eyes on but weren't able to afford, until now. After signing for Bristol I decided to go for broke and I went straight out and bought one of those new houses.

Not long after that I also treated myself to a

Mercedes to replace my Peugeot 206. It felt so good to be able to afford these things and for a while I splashed out on new clothes, holidays and other little treats. A lot of it was keeping up with the Jones' as the boys at Bristol all had nice stuff and I didn't want to be left behind. I even bought myself an Aquascutum wash bag as I noticed that all the boys had designer ones. After all my hard graft I also felt that I deserved to spoil myself but whilst it was fine going a bit mad at first, I eventually started living way beyond my means. In the end, as you will see, all this materialistic crap swallowed me up.

Fulfilling my dream move to a big club was a great feeling but leaving Exeter was hard. I enjoyed my time in Devon and made some lifelong friends. Due to the speed of my transfer to Bristol City I hadn't been able to say goodbye to everyone but as luck would have it, a few days after my move, Exeter had a fixture at Bristol Rovers so I went along. The Rovers fans immediately recognised me in the stands, and some abuse flew about, but that didn't bother me. I gave them a wink and a smile and it amused me to see them all get so wound up. After the match I went down to the changing room and gave the boys a few crates of beer, as a gesture of my thanks to them, and I have to admit I was a bit emotional. Despite feeling sad that my time at Exeter had come to an end I was invigorated thinking about the challenge that lay ahead of me at my new club.

The first day at any new club is just like the first day at school. It's exciting but nerve racking and I hoped it would go without a hitch. So imagine how I felt when as soon as I turned up the lads absolutely slaughtered me. At the time I had a shaved head and a goatee and as I was being introduced to the players Scott Murray piped up, 'Fucking hell. We've signed Fabian Barthez'. I laughed and it broke the ice but then, for the rest of training, I was christened 'Fabian'!

The lads had a game against Reading that night but I wasn't eligible to play. Sitting in the stands, sucking in the atmosphere that 17,000 fans can provide, and watching the standard of football got me excited. I couldn't wait to play in front of those fans and get a taste of it all.

My debut for Bristol City was away to Brighton in what was a must-win game. There were only four games left in the season and we needed to win the majority of them to guarantee ourselves a place in the play offs.

The night before the Brighton game I was sat on the bed watching TV with my roommate Steve Robinson, when there was a knock on the door. Robbo opened the door and let in a number of Bristol City players. On entering the room they said, 'We've come to welcome Christian to the club and to make sure everything is alright'.

We had a bit of a chat and all the boys seemed really nice and willing to help. They all left after 10 minutes and I remember telling Robbo, 'That was nice of them. They seem a good bunch of lads'.

Not long after this we both smelt something stinking out the room. We looked around for a while but we couldn't find where it was coming from. I finally realised that one of the lamps absolutely reeked. On closer inspection of the lamp I soon realised what the smell was, one of the players had placed some shit inside it and it was burning on the bulb. I couldn't believe it.

Robbo then shouted from the bathroom, 'Chris. You better take a look at this!' I walked into the bathroom to find it in a state and to top it all, one of them had pissed in my new designer wash bag. The Bristol City boys had just introduced me to their unique form of banter. Whilst I was determined to get my own back I was quickly warned that those lads would keep going if I did anything back to them so I decided to chin it and bide my time.

It was true though, the lads at Bristol were nuts. I know a lot is made of the Crazy Gang at Wimbledon but I doubt whether even those boys could compete with some of the stuff I saw during my time at Bristol. Despite this I became close to the chief troublemakers and we regularly socialised, but I tried to stay well clear of some of their pranks as they were mental.

Not only was Bristol City a step up in class but it was also a step up in drinking. The drinking culture was massive and we would all regularly go on the piss together. The rule on our nights out was that if it was your round you chose what the group drank and everyone had to down it. At the start of the night the drinks were something easy going like a round of Buds. Then it would progress to a cocktail and perhaps a pint and a shot. It deteriorated until we could barely stand.

I remember once that some idiot bought us all a bottle of wine. We had to neck a whole bottle of the stuff and then had a vodka chaser to follow. This wasn't out of the ordinary—our drinking was way out of hand but we were young men who thought we were invincible.

On those nights out we all ended up in some horrific states. One night I took all the boys out in Cardiff with me. There was an argument between a player and our designated driver of the night, which led to the player leaving the pub in a sulk for a bit. We returned to our car some time later to discover that the angry player had shat all over the windscreen!

There were constant stitch ups amongst the boys as well. We were always winding each other up or cutting up each other's clothes. It was a madhouse of young men high on life.

It wasn't just drink that we all loved. We all enjoyed a bet and had a bit of a card school going on. Before away games we would be on the bus, or in a hotel, playing three-card brag for silly money. There were plenty of times that one of us blew his week's wages on cards before a game. It didn't really put you in a good frame of mind to play after that as you were left thinking, 'Shit! My other half better not find out otherwise she's going to go nuts'.

Despite all this craziness there was a bunch of talented footballers playing at Bristol during this time. Football always came first; we trained unbelievably hard and gave our all on the pitch. Everyone associated with the club was desperate for promotion but unfortunately it was not to be.

During my debut against Brighton I thought I had opened my Bristol City account when I unleashed a rocket from 30 yards. The ball seemed destined for the top corner, and as I was about to run away and celebrate, the keeper got his fingertips onto the ball and tipped it over the bar. We ended up losing the game 2–1, and whilst we beat Bury in the next game, we were then thrashed 5–1 by Blackpool to end any hopes we had of reaching the play offs. After that game the dressing room was like a morgue, the boys were all slumped in their seats, no one saying a word. I was, of course, disappointed but I didn't feel anywhere near the devastation that the rest of the team were feeling. After all, I had only signed with four league games remaining so I personally never quite felt as if I was involved in a promotion chase.

The day after crashing to Blackpool we had the PFA awards to attend in London. All footballers always look forward to the PFA awards, as it's a good opportunity to blow off some steam with those in your profession. On the Saturday night I stayed at my teammate, Lee Peacock's house, and we went on a mad 24-hour binge with the rest of the team. After the Blackpool result everyone was in need of a good drink to take their mind off things and we certainly did that.

During the PFA awards one thing was definitely on everyone's minds—one way or another we would get promoted the following season.

8

ALCOHOL TAKES
A GRIP

The 2002–03 season was one of the happiest, and darkest, times in both my career and personal life. On the pitch everything was going well, I was playing regularly and scoring goals in a successful team, but off it the wheels had started to come off. This was the year where alcoholism grabbed hold of me with a firm grip and refused to let go until it had shredded all my dignity.

Ironically, in spite of the spectre of drink being constantly present, this season turned out to be the most productive of my career. During that first pre-season with Bristol I started to appreciate how much of a step up the club was from Exeter. The players were better, the training facilities were fantastic, the pitches were always top notch and even the kit was nicer. The club even had a guy called Ken on the coach, after away games, to cook us things like scrambled egg and beans and toast.

Danny Wilson had also assembled a good backroom staff who not only advised on tactical aspects of the game but also on other aspects such as diet and recovery drinks. This was all a new experience to me, at Exeter everything was hard but at Bristol it all came a little easier.

During that pre-season I was also introduced to 7–10–2. In other words we would be up at 7.00am to do a 40-minute run. At 10.00am we would do yardage running and at 2.00pm we would then do ball work. It was hard work but by the end of that summer I was in great shape and raring to go.

The league was a tough one that year with teams such as Wigan, QPR, Cardiff and Crewe all spending big money, and having strong squads, so we knew we were in for a hard season. Despite vowing to be all guns blazing for promotion we actually started the season indifferently with a few wins and a few defeats. I opened my Bristol City account with a goal against Wycombe and followed that up with a goal against Chesterfield when we thrashed them 4–0. I was feeling confident in my ability and I had no doubts that I had what it took to be a player at this level.

Following the Chesterfield game we played Barnsley away and I scored the first, and only, hat-trick of my career. It was a perfect hat-trick as well with the goals scored from my left foot, right foot and then from a header. The team was well into its stride, after a difficult start, and we went 17 games unbeaten as we marched up the table. I managed to score 10 goals in that spell so I felt that I was making a good contribution to our promotion push.

We also had a nice run in the FA Cup when we reached the third round and secured a nice draw against Championship side Leicester City at the Walkers Stadium. I had never played a team from the

Championship before so I was eager to test myself against better players.

FA Cup weekend is always special to me and I hate it when people rubbish the Cup because it is such a great competition. Every time I played an FA Cup tie I always thought about being a kid and watching the build up to the Final. By being involved in such a competition, even at its early stages, I would dream about maybe getting through all the rounds and playing in a Cup Final myself, after all this was the competition of the underdog.

Whilst our dreams of an upset didn't come true at Leicester, as we lost 2–0, we put up a good account of ourselves. I was also pleased with my own performance and felt I had shown that, if I was ever given the opportunity, I could play at a higher level. It was also a thrill to play in a big, modern stadium, like the Walkers, in front of 30,000 fans. The noise from the fans gave me goose pimples and I wondered what it must be like to play in a stadium like that every week.

The only downside of that game at Leicester was that I picked up my fifth booking of the season, which meant I would be suspended for our top of the table clash against Wigan. I was annoyed when I heard I had accumulated five bookings, as the club statisticians were sure that it was only my fourth, until they did some checks and realised that they had forgotten to count one of my earlier cards.

I loved my football during this time, particularly playing at Ashton Gate. Driving up the M4 to Bristol on a match day, in my Mercedes, with my music on full volume really got me in the mood. Upon arriving at Ashton Gate there would always be hordes of fans waiting for autographs and I signed as many as I could before going into the changing room to see my kit laid out for me. The lads would all be in there and we would have a spot of mickey taking, usually over Danny Wilson's dodgy suede Gucci shoes, then one of the boys would belt on some tunes and we would all get our heads on the game ahead. Running out in front of 15,000–20,000 fans every home game was an unreal experience and I used to feed off their noise. It all gave me a real buzz. The whole experience of playing for Bristol City was an absolute honour.

The only thing that bugged me about playing at Bristol was Danny Wilson's tendency to take me off after around 65 minutes in almost every game. It didn't matter if I was playing well or not I would still be substituted. Bristol City had an abundance of strikers that season with Lee Peacock, Lee Matthews, Mark Robins on loan and me so I suppose Danny wanted to give everyone a game, but it did my head in and just as I would be feeling my way into a game I would be dragged off. Despite this frustration I was still enjoying being a part of Bristol City and it was something I learned to put up with.

Whilst I enjoyed my football at this time there was something that I loved more. Alcohol. As I said previously, there was a drinking culture at Bristol City so alcohol was steadily becoming a big influence in my life, and before I knew it I couldn't do without it. I don't blame the nights out with the lads at Bristol City for setting me off. I feel that alcoholism was always buried deep inside me and was like a ticking time bomb ready to explode. I believe I was born an alcoholic, both my grandfather and my mother had their problems with alcohol, and it was only a matter of time before I also fell victim to a similar fate.

During my first year at Bristol I started incorporating drink into absolutely everything that I did. If I was having a carvery with the family on a Sunday I demolished five pints of Stella before lunch. On cinema trips with Janine I insisted on sitting in the Gallery seats so that I could have a drink. One time, when we went to watch *Bad Boys 2*, I was so steaming that I could barely see the screen and ended up falling into a drink-induced coma in my chair. If I went out to hire a DVD from Blockbuster I nipped into the pub for half an hour to neck as many pints as I could before Janine started asking questions about why I took so long. If she ever did ask I would say I had bumped into a friend.

That's what alcohol addiction does, it forces you to become an excellent actor and liar to cover the amount of alcohol that you are consuming. So that Janine wasn't able to keep tracks on my drinking, I hid booze all over the place so I could have a cheeky swig when she wasn't around. For instance I would tell her that I was playing online poker in our room upstairs, but I would hide bottles of wine in the cupboard and get through two or three bottles at a time. I developed an unquenchable, burning thirst for alcohol and no matter how much I drank I was never satisfied.

In previous years I rarely went out on Saturday nights, as I would prefer to sit in with Janine, have a few drinks and watch some TV, but this season I started to go out almost every weekend. If I went out on a Saturday sometimes I wouldn't return home for two or three days as I continued to drink until I collapsed. I usually drank right through the Saturday night and early on Sunday morning I would go to the off-license and buy a six-pack of Stella. At 10.00am I was usually stood in a park watching Sunday league football matches whilst steadily drinking can after can. Sometimes I even had Ethan with me but that didn't stop me drinking in front of him. What sort of example must I have been setting? I lost complete respect for being a family man.

When I was Ethan's age I hated my Mum for letting alcohol rule her life and I'm sure Ethan must have wondered what the hell his Dad was doing. I had seen the effects that alcohol could have on a person, and a family, close hand, yet that still didn't deter me from following my Mum's path to full blown alcoholism.

Over the years I had always enjoyed a beer or two on a Friday night to help me relax but Friday nights now became full-scale drinking marathons. On Saturday I would play either drunk or hungover but somehow I got away with it and still delivered decent performances. It was only later that drink really started to affect how I played.

I don't know how my body actually allowed me to play professional football. There was never a point when I was playing or training when I did not have alcohol in my system. We regularly had games on a Tuesday night and I played when I was still out of my skull, I had no business being on a football pitch yet somehow, at this stage, I was getting away with it.

My level of training was ridiculous; every day I ran off a hangover and sweated out alcohol. After all-night sessions I would still be drunk and virtually falling asleep in training, if I actually turned up at all. Some days I woke up with a raging hangover and decided that I needed to spend the whole day drinking to sort myself out. If this were the case I would call Danny Wilson and tell him that I couldn't go in, because I had family issues to sort out, and he would let me have the day off. Danny Wilson was a smashing bloke and I have no doubt that he would have helped me in any way that he could but I did everything in my power to hide my alcohol issues from him, including repeatedly lying to his face.

The days when I did attend training I was eager to get away as quickly as possible so that I could return to the pub. As soon as training finished at midday I raced to my car, bombed it down the M4 to Cardiff to be sat in the pub having a drink by 1.00pm.

At 2.00pm I would call Janine from the pub and say that I was doing some extra training in Bristol and would be leaving soon. That would buy me some more time so I could continue my quest to get as smashed as possible. If necessary I would happily drink by myself but I would prefer to sit with the painters and decorators who were enjoying a pint on their lunch break. Even though I was a footballer, I still considered myself to be working class, and if I hadn't turned professional I have no doubt that I would have been a builder or something like that and I was always more comfortable in that type of company.

It was like I was living two lives, everyone thought I was a clean living professional footballer but I was a chronic alcoholic. There was not a moment when I was not burning inside for another drink and I did everything in my power to make sure that alcohol was always close at hand.

A guy called Gary, who I saw in the pub every day, remarked once that I was drinking a lot and I cockily replied, 'Well so are you'. He explained that whilst he did like a drink, he was in control of the amount he drank and could stop whenever he wanted. I said that I was in control as well and stopping would not be a problem for me. After a brief discussion we agreed that we would go an entire month without alcohol to show that we could control our drinking. We typically picked February, because it is the shortest month, and after a heavy January we sat down on 1st February and ordered the fruit soft drink, J2O. The next day we had the same again, and he seemed quite happy, but my insides were leaping up and down yearning for some alcohol. By 3rd February I snapped and guzzled as much booze as I could. Fair play to Gary, he went the whole month without drinking and proved that he could happily go without alcohol. I didn't even stop to consider whether I was in control or not, I wanted to get drunk.

I had entered professional football as the alcohol culture was leaving the game and the foreign managers and players came in to set an example regarding how to prepare professionally. Yet I was still living my life as a lot of footballers did in the 1980s, where most players enjoyed a drink and no one questioned the effect that it would have on performance. If, for a brief moment, I thought about how much I was drinking I lied to myself and decided that I needed a drink to help me unwind. In the end alcohol became a great leveller, it didn't pick me up, it made me feel normal.

Despite having signed a decent contract at Bristol,

earning more than double what I had earned at Exeter, I was constantly broke. Virtually every single penny that I made went on alcohol. It was ridiculous. I spent all my wages, maxed out credit cards and took out loans to keep up with my addiction. Not once did I question whether things were getting out of hand.

Another issue that arose, because of my drinking and having a bit of success, was that I felt that I was this big time footballer and I had to be seen to be living that kind of lifestyle. I spent money I didn't have on cars, clothes and anything else that took my fancy to project a certain image. Yes, I was earning decent money but nowhere near enough to live that sort of life. My Dad's lesson to work hard, and only buy what you can afford, was by now a distant memory.

My attitude also became a problem and I started to behave like some big time Charlie. During one game, away to play off rivals QPR, we were losing 1–0 and I wasn't having the best of games when Peter Beadle came on for us. Peter was an experienced professional at the club and as he came onto the field he had a pop at me. I instantly told him to go fuck himself. Here I was, no more than 23 years of age, having a go at a respected professional like Peter Beadle. Peter doesn't take any messing, and he's a big strong bloke as well, so he answered back, 'Go fuck myself? I'll see you in the changing room after the game', and he did! As soon as we got in there he went for me and the players had to separate us. I didn't give a shit at the time, I thought, 'Who the hell is a has-been like him to have a go at me?' That was my attitude back then.

As I said before, arrogance can be a healthy thing for a footballer as long as it is channelled in the right direction. If you look at some of the great players over the last few years such as Eric Cantona, Cristiano Ronaldo and Thierry Henry it's fair to say that they all had a bit of arrogance about them but it helped make them believe in themselves. Previously my arrogance had been good for me but now it was channelled in the wrong direction. I was too full of myself, even though I had hardly done a thing in the game, and I was too quick to blame others for my shortcomings.

Even though I was drinking heavily I was still delivering on the pitch and that season provided me with one of the most memorable games of my career. During the team's winning streak we were faced with the prospect of playing our promotion rivals, Cardiff City at Ninian Park. Cardiff City had been promoted to the same division as Bristol the year before, following Sam Hammam's spending spree. They were one of the glamour teams in the division as they were big spenders and had a squad that was the envy of most teams.

Bristol City and Cardiff have always had a fierce rivalry and it seemed particularly intense back then, probably because Cardiff hadn't really had many derby games with Swansea in recent years, due to being in different divisions, so this contest had somewhat taken its place. As both clubs were also fighting for promotion there was also a lot of hype surrounding the game.

The fact that I was returning to Cardiff City, as a Bristol City player, in a big game also seemed to add some spice to the occasion. I did interviews for the media almost every day the week before the clash and my comments to the press stoked up the pre-match atmosphere: 'I probably shouldn't be saying this but I can't wait. I have to be honest—if there's going to be a game that I have got to score in or have a good game it is this one. It was an acrimonious departure, which was through two people. There was Billy Ayre who wanted me out of the club. And before that Frank Burrows came into the club and gave me a three-year contract and he never played me.'

Unfortunately most of the staff that had made my life hell at Cardiff had left by now so I couldn't show them how wrong they had been about me. Despite this I was still looking forward to showing those in my hometown that I was a good player and could play at this level. I still had friends at the club, such as some of the match day staff, and players like Andy Legg, Jason Bowen and Earnie so I was looking forward to seeing them all, but at the same time I was determined to put one over on them.

Before the game I bumped into Nathan Blake, who had been a legend at Cardiff, and was now playing for Wolves. Blakey had some experience of going back to Ninian Park with another team and he warned me not to wind up the crowd or react to any abuse. As I still lived in Cardiff he said that I didn't need any aggro as it would only take one idiot to do me some serious damage when I least expected it.

The game was played on Saturday 14 December 2002 so it was bitterly cold, and the match was played under floodlights. Before the game the atmosphere was crackling. I remember the Cardiff fans pelting our team bus with missiles outside the ground and them screaming abuse at us as we stepped off it. When we went out to warm up, Ninian Park was full and the Bob Bank was crackling. We had our little mob of fans in the corner of the Grange End and they were singing their hearts out trying to be heard above the Ninian Park din.

As I was warming up at the Grange End I heard some of the Cardiff fans slagging me off and then someone threw a coin at me. That really upset me because I was a Cardiff boy and a Cardiff City fan. I had wanted to spend my entire career at the club but I was bombed out, it wasn't my fault that I wasn't wearing the blue of Cardiff that day. Although the fans who were abusing me had no idea what had gone on during my time there, I was still furious. It really wound me up but Nathan Blake's words were ringing in my head so I didn't react.

When we went back into the changing room, after warming up, I was like a bear with a sore ass. I kept repeating to myself, 'This is going to be it! This is going to be it! I'm going to put everything to rest today!' I was so vexed I almost needed someone to calm me down.

The game went by in a flash, and it's all a bit of a blur now, but I remember that Brian Tinion had put us 1–0 up, via a penalty, and then in the second half my moment of redemption came in front of the Grange End. Neil Alexander, the Cardiff goalkeeper, miss-kicked a clearance, which fell straight at my feet. All that was left for me to do was to pass the ball past him into the Cardiff goal to put us 2–0 up.

It was strange because I thought that if I scored against Cardiff I would go mental but as soon as the ball went in I didn't want to celebrate. I was ecstatic to score in the circumstances but Cardiff had been my team, I still had friends at the club and a lot of my friends and family were Cardiff fans so I made an instant decision not to celebrate. I always used to say back then that I didn't give a fuck about Cardiff, after the way I had been treated, but inside I still loved them. However, if Billy Ayre had been in the dug out I would have run in front of him swinging my shirt above my head.

After the game I revealed my mixed feelings about the goal to the media: 'It's been an emotional week and I was a bit surprised at the reception I got because in 10 years at Cardiff I never let the club down. I still come back to watch them if I've got an evening off because I supported them as a boy. It's probably the only goal in my career that I didn't enjoy scoring. I had to do it but I couldn't celebrate. I did nothing in that game to get the fans against me and we came to get the result.'

Whilst the match took place over eight years ago, people in Cardiff still talk to me about not celebrating my goal. From that game on I got a lot of respect from those Cardiff fans that had been giving me stick, which is probably for the best as I still lived in the city.

I wasn't just happy with the outcome of the game for myself though, I was pleased for everyone connected with Bristol City as not only had we won a local derby but we had also strengthened our promotion push. As I walked off the pitch some Cardiff fans still weren't happy with me and told me that if they saw me out that night I would get my face slashed. I had actually planned to meet up with Andy Legg and Jason Bowen for a night out but decided that it probably wouldn't be the best idea considering the circumstances.

In the end I went to my local, The Village Inn, with all my friends and family who had been at the game.

Even though there were around 20 of us there that didn't stop one idiot mouthing off and trying to start a fight with me. Thankfully he was soon warned in no uncertain terms by my entourage that he needed to shut up and leave.

In the return fixture against Cardiff, at Ashton Gate, we again won 2–0 and once again I got my name on the score sheet. This time I did do a little aeroplane celebration with both my arms outstretched before remembering who I had scored against and swiftly stopped.

Those goals seemed to exorcise some of the demons I had been carrying around in my head. After what had gone on with Billy Ayre I had been carrying a huge chip on my shoulder for some time but with my goals and performances I believe I showed everyone that he was wrong not to give me a chance at Cardiff.

In between our promotion push, we had a great run in the LDV Vans Trophy, which saw us reach the Final where we met Carlisle United. The Final was to be played, out of all the places, at the Millennium Stadium in Cardiff. You can't imagine how excited I was to play there. It is the dream of every footballer to play in their national stadium, and I was thrilled to be playing in a Final in front of all my family and friends.

Walking out on that field, with 40,000 Bristol fans singing their hearts out, made me so proud. As I was the Cardiff boy, returning home, everyone tipped me to be the match winner and I was convinced that it would be my day. Unfortunately I was atrocious and I was subbed after 70 minutes to make way for Leroy Lita. What really shocked me, and the rest of the boys, was how poor the pitch was at the Millennium Stadium. It cut up easily and the grass was too long, which made running with the ball and passing difficult. I'm not making excuses for my abysmal performance but it really didn't help. Thankfully we won the game 2–1 and I enjoyed celebrating a Cup win at my national stadium.

There was cause for further celebration as the season was coming to an end as Janine gave birth to our second son, Ewan. Obviously I was ecstatic, especially after what we had both been through previously, and I was such a proud Dad. The only difference this time, compared to when Ethan was born, was that I was by now a full-blown alcoholic and it's sad to say it but alcohol came before anything else, including my new baby boy.

Whilst our form was decent going into the end of the season we had dropped vital points, at places like our play off rivals QPR, and that meant we had to settle for a place in the play offs rather than achieve automatic promotion. I'll never forget how my heart sank when I was told that we had drawn Cardiff in the play off semis. I knew that after already beating them twice that season, and having scored against them on both occasions, they would have their revenge.

We lost the first game at Ninian Park 1–0 but I would have levelled the scores if Neil Alexander had not made an outstanding save from my looping header. Losing 1–0 wasn't a disaster and I was confident that we could turn them over at Ashton Gate.

To be honest we battered Cardiff in the return fixture but they put 11 men behind the ball and defended on their 18-yard line to squeeze all the space behind them. We had all the possession but couldn't break them down. The game ended 0–0 and our season was over. We were facing yet another season in League One. Cardiff went on to get promoted, after beating QPR in the play off final, and I was gutted as I honestly thought we were a better team than them that season. We had the nucleus of a very good side and if we had been promoted I'm sure we would have done well in the Championship.

Despite the play off disappointment my first full season for Bristol had been a success as I had won a trophy and finished the season with 17 goals. If I had played primarily up front I would have scored even more but Danny played me on both wings, and in the hole, as well as up top. However the pain of missing out on promotion for the second season running stung both the team and me badly and we were understandably feeling low.

However, whilst not reaching the play off final was tough, it did present me with an opportunity I thought I would never get in my career.

9

REPORTING
FOR DUTY

Whilst I was, of course, bitterly disappointed to lose in the play off semi-finals, it did provide me with an unexpected opportunity. That summer Wales were due to play the USA in San Jose, California. The rumour was that if Bristol beat Cardiff in the play off semi then Earnie would get a call up whilst if Cardiff beat us, which of course they did, then I would get called up.

Shortly after losing that play off semi game I received a phone call that confirmed the rumour, I was in the Welsh squad! I couldn't believe that I was going to get the chance to win a cap. Throughout my time in football the senior Welsh team had always seemed to elude me so I was really looking forward to making the most of my opportunity.

Despite Ryan Giggs and Craig Bellamy not travelling with the squad we still had some talented players with us. There was Gary Speed, Mark Pembridge, Jason Koumas and Andy Melville to name a few.

The day before we were scheduled to fly to the USA from Heathrow the squad met up at the Marriott hotel in Slough. As soon as I walked in the Welsh kitman, Quaggs, sorted me out with the kit and I couldn't wait to get my Welsh tracksuit on. I ran straight up to my hotel room, changed into all the gear, and spent a long time admiring myself in the mirror. There I was looking and feeling like an international footballer. I couldn't believe it!

The squad met downstairs for dinner at around 8.00pm and after that most of us headed to the hotel bar for a nightcap. I instantly latched on to some of the experienced players in the squad who were having a good drink. It was clear that whilst we were on international duty, some of the lads weren't taking it as seriously as perhaps they would a qualifier and that was evident by how much drink they were putting away. I didn't need a second invitation, I was in my element amongst them all, so I got stuck in.

By about 1.00am most of the lads had gone to bed but I was still going strong. It was ridiculous really, I was a youngster, on the first day of his international call up, and I was getting pissed. For some reason I thought that it was acceptable for me to sit with all of these great, respected international players, who had done so much in the game, and do exactly what they were all doing. Eventually Mark Hughes, the manager, walked into the bar to see me sitting there still drinking away and he half jokingly said, 'I can see who you've linked yourself up with'. I assume he meant that I had immediately sat down with the heavier drinkers in the squad but that didn't deter me from having a few more drinks. I finally retired in the early hours and I was wasted.

The next day we flew to San Jose and checked into our hotel. We were meant to have a quiet night but some of us found a bar next to the hotel and had a few drinks. My few drinks turned into a lot and again I was hammered. I had spent my first two days with the Welsh squad getting trolleyed.

During our week in the USA I think I got wasted every single day, apart from the night before the game, but even then I managed to sneak a few drinks to keep the alcohol in my system. On two of the nights I sneaked out of the team hotel by myself, when everyone else had gone to bed, and went to the bar nearby to get my fix. As I went to that bar so often I soon got to know all the staff, as they would speak to me whilst I drank alone.

Due to the hot weather, and the eight hour time difference, it was decided that we would train in the late afternoon so that at least gave me some time to sober up. However, the extent of my drinking was taking its toll on my performances in training, as I would be working off a hangover and sweating out buckets of alcohol in the searing heat. When you are up against top quality international players it's hard enough anyway, let alone when you feel like shit, and whilst I didn't humiliate myself I didn't play anywhere near as well as I could have done. God knows what Mark Hughes must have thought of me!

Another incident that probably didn't do me any favours was when we went as a squad to watch a baseball game. Before the game I went to the team's club shop and bought myself a huge inflatable hat and a foam hand. We weren't allowed to drink at the game, but I still had alcohol in my system, so I was loud and making a scene in my new attire. Mark Hughes was watching but I didn't care, I wanted to have fun regardless of the behaviour that was expected of me. Whilst I was at the game I even bumped into some Bristol City supporters. What must they have thought when they saw me like that?

When the starting 11 was announced for our game against the USA I wasn't particularly surprised when I was named amongst the substitutes. As long as I got on the pitch I would get a cap, and could call myself an international footballer, so that was what I was pinning my hopes on. With around 25 minutes remaining Mark Hughes told me to go warm up, which I took as a sign that I was going on. I could barely wait to get out on that pitch and warmed up on the sidelines like a mad man ready for my big moment. Yet as I was warming up Matthew Jones was sent off and I was told to sit back down in the dug out. It was clear that I would not be going on and I was absolutely gutted. So close yet still so far. The boys on the pitch put up a good fight but with 10 men, playing in the heat, it was difficult for them and we lost the game 1–0.

Despite the crushing disappointment of not getting a cap I was still determined to enjoy myself that night. We went out as a squad to the bar I had been secretly sneaking to during the week and I proceeded to get stuck into the booze. After I had a few beers I became a bit lairy and whilst speaking to the bar owner, I demanded that he should allow me behind the bar to serve drinks. Unbelievably he let me. I put on one of the bar's baseball caps backwards and started serving the Welsh boys beers, shots, champagne and all sorts. I started to think I was Tom Cruise in *Cocktail* so when Mark Hughes walked in, and stood at the end of the bar, I slid a beer along the counter towards him like you see in films, thinking I was the bollocks.

As the beer slid towards Hughesy he looked up to see one of his players, off his face, behind the bar. He did not look amused and who could blame him? He walked towards me, with that steely stare of his focussing on me, and through gritted teeth, said 'Behave yourself. Calm down!' No chance! It didn't matter that this was the manager of the national team telling me to sort myself out, the barriers were down and I wanted to get annihilated.

It was no surprise whatsoever that I never received another international call up. If I had been Mark Hughes there is no way I would have called up someone like me again so I can't blame him. Obviously I would have loved an international cap but I try to live my life without regrets. It's those type of experiences that have made me who I am today. You certainly learn from your mistakes, although it would take me a while to learn from this particular lesson.

After the disappointment of missing out on the play offs, and not getting a cap, I was delighted when Janine and I finally got married in Jamaica that summer. We had been together for around six years and now had two kids so it was only right that we officially became a family by getting married. My alcoholism had caused some friction over the last year but I think we were both hoping that perhaps marriage would calm me down. It didn't, it simply made my descent into a full scale, raging alcoholic even deeper and darker than it had ever been before.

10

THE DESCENT

After a season of so many highs and lows I was confident that 2003–04 was going to be the year when Bristol City finally sealed promotion to the Championship. We had come desperately close over the previous two seasons but after those disappointments there was an unbelievable hunger throughout the squad to do it at any cost that year.

Everything seemed in place for us virtually to guarantee promotion and confidence was high. We had a strong squad, with a good mixture of youth and experience, a forward thinking manager, a dynamic backroom staff and a chairman willing to invest in the team if he thought it necessary. As a gambling man I would have bet everything I owned that we would get promoted.

My drinking had been hardcore the previous year but I had somehow managed to have a productive season. However, this year my drinking really took its toll on my performances and I found myself in and out of the team. I was like a man possessed by this point; nothing whatsoever mattered in my world apart from drinking. I had worked hard to become a professional footballer but I was steadily becoming a disgrace, not only to my profession, but also to my family and all those fans that paid good money to watch me play.

There is no finer example of how bad my drinking had become than when we played Watford at Ashton Gate, in the League Cup, on Tuesday 23 September 2003. I had gone out with Janine on the Saturday and as usual I drank until I was shit faced. We had some sort of argument, I was so drunk I can't even recall what it was over, but no doubt it started because I was becoming obnoxious. The disagreement with my wife was cutting into my valuable drinking time so I walked off and left her in town by herself. I honestly can't recall where I ended up, or who I saw, all I know is that I carried on drinking as much as I possibly could. The next morning I was waiting at The Carpenters Arms pub in Cardiff for it to open so I could continue drinking and as I waited I calmed my thirst with a few cans of Stella.

I spent all day Sunday drinking in The Carpenters Arms and then went off somewhere else to carry on throughout the night. My memory is hazy as to where I went, as I was so far gone. On the Monday, not only was I too hammered to go to training, but also my thirst for alcohol was still burning so I rang Danny Wilson and told him I wasn't going to make training due to some family problems. With a day off secured, I went straight up the pub and stayed until it closed and then went into town to hit some clubs. At 11.00am on Tuesday morning I finally returned home and I was off my face. As I staggered through the door I remember for some reason that my Dad was in the house and he stared at me in disbelief. I ignored him and collapsed in bed.

After a few hours sleep I drove myself to Bristol. I was still so drunk I could barely walk straight and I had no business being behind the wheel of a car. When I got to Ashton Gate I went to see Danny Wilson to explain why I had missed training. As soon as he saw me he looked concerned and said, 'Are you in a fit state to play?' I desperately wanted to say 'No' but for some reason I told him that I was all right.

During the game I felt like shit. My heart was racing, I was sweating out three days' worth of alcohol, I had barely slept and I was still absolutely hammered. I was an embarrassment, my touch was like a pub player's, and at times I almost fell flat on my face, I was having the worst game of my entire life. For some reason Danny didn't take me off, maybe he was trying to teach me a lesson but I was dying out there. To top it all off the game went to extra time so I played 120 minutes blind drunk. The only saving grace was that we managed to win the game 1–0 but the boys worked their socks off to cover for me and it must have been like playing with 10 men. As soon as the final whistle went I ran straight off the pitch, into the players bar, and greedily guzzled another pint.

Even after that experience it still wasn't a wake up call to seek help. I don't know how I did it but I managed to hide the full extent of my drinking problem from my teammates and the manager. Of course they knew I liked a drink but who didn't at Bristol? I'm sure that if anyone had known how bad my dependency on alcohol had become then they would have dragged me kicking and screaming to rehab but even if they had I would have left and found the nearest boozer.

The sad thing is we had a fantastic psychologist at Bristol called Brian Jones and he really helped to motivate some of the lads and deal with any personal issues they may have had. A lot of the boys swore by him but he couldn't help me as every time I saw him I lied. He didn't know the dark world I now inhabited so there was nothing he could offer that could sort out my problems.

The team was doing well, and we were in the top six for most of the season, but my performances were getting progressively worse. In the first 38 games of the season I had managed to score a grand total of two goals. As a result Danny Wilson dropped me, and brought in players on loan. I was of course furious and took it out on our coach, Frank Barlow. Frank was a lovely guy and he did his best to keep my confidence high but with me being out of the first 11, I saw this as an excuse to drink even harder as I didn't need to be fit for 90 minutes.

However, when the loan players returned to their clubs I suddenly found myself back in the first team picture with the business end of the season coming up. I don't know how it happened, as I was still drinking hard, but for some reason my form suddenly came together and every shot I took seemed to hit the back of the net. Earlier in the season I couldn't buy a goal, and nothing would go in, but now I was not only playing well but I also had that all important element of luck.

In the last seven games of the season I scored five goals which was enough to propel us into the play off semi-finals for a second straight season. We missed out on automatic promotion by a solitary point and in those circumstances you can't help thinking about all the times someone has missed a chance, or made a defensive mistake, which led to dropping silly points. I hold my hands up and admit that my spell of two goals in 38 games certainly didn't do us any favours but for some reason the game that kept coming back to me was when we drew 1–1 with Swindon and Lee Miller somehow missed an open goal on the line. Of course you can't say that it was all Lee Miller's fault that we didn't go straight up—throughout the season every player had made some sort of costly error. But that missed chance stuck in my head. Sorry Lee, it was an absolute shocker!

With us back in the play offs we were all determined that this would be our year and I was going to do everything in my power to fire us up. From being an outcast Danny Wilson was now telling me, 'You can make a name for yourself. You can get us promoted!'

For us to reach the play off final we would firstly have to overcome Hartlepool in the semis. We played the first leg at Victoria Road and the game finished 1–1. The tie was now very much in our favour as we prepared to face them at Ashton Gate and I was sure that we would have enough to see them off.

Before the game, psychologist Brian Jones made a motivational DVD to help put us in the right frame of mind. He had put together footage of our finest moments from that season set to Al Pacino's speech in the film *Any Given Sunday*. The words mean so much to me that I have put them below for you to read for yourself. In fact at one point I was even considering trying to get the whole speech tattooed down my back, as I do honestly believe it is one of the finest motivational speeches I have ever heard. Obviously Al Pacino's passionate delivery of these words really makes them come alive but I still think that you can feel the adrenalin that they create by reading them:

I don't know what to say really. Three minutes till the biggest battle of our professional lives. It all comes down to today. Now either we heal as a team, or we're gonna crumble. Inch by inch, play by play, till we're finished. We're in hell right now, gentlemen. Believe me. And we can stay here, get the shit kicked out of us, or we can fight our way back into the light. We can climb out of hell. One inch at a time.

Now I can't do it for you. I'm too old. I look around, I see these young faces, and I think . . . I mean I've made every wrong choice a middle-aged man can make. I pissed away all my money, believe it or not. I chased off anyone who's ever loved me, and lately, I can't even stand the face I see in the mirror. You know when you get old in life, things get taken from you. That's part of life. But you only learn that when you start losing stuff. You find out life's this game of inches. And so is football. Because in either game, life or football, the margin for error is so small. I mean . . . one half a step too late or too early and you don't quite make it. One half second too slow or too fast, you don't quite catch it. The inches we need are everywhere around us. They are in every break of the game, every minute, every second. On this team, we fight for that inch. On this team, we tear ourselves and everyone else around us to pieces for that inch. We claw with our fingernails for that inch. Because we know when we add up all those inches, that's gonna make the fucking difference between winning and losing! Between living and dying! I'll tell you this—in any fight, it's the guy who's willing to die who's gonna win that inch. And I know if I'm going to have any life anymore, it's because I'm still willing to fight and die for that inch. Because that's what living is! The six inches in front of your face.

Now I can't make you do it. You've got to look at the

guy next to you, look into his eyes. Now I think you're gonna see a guy who will go that inch with you. You're gonna see a guy who will sacrifice himself for this team, because he knows when it comes down to it, you're gonna do the same for him.

That's a team, gentlemen. And either we heal, now, as a team, or we will die, as individuals. That's football, guys. That's all it is. Now, what are you going to do?

By the end of that segment of the DVD I was literally punching the walls as I was psyched up out of my mind, but then somehow Brian Jones took the motivation up another notch. The next segment of the DVD was more footage of us playing set to the song, 'Lose Yourself' by Eminem. The song is all about having one chance to make your dreams come true with lyrics such as: 'If you had one shot or one opportunity to seize everything you ever wanted, one moment, could you capture it? Or let it slip?'

As the baseline was kicking into that song, and those words were swirling around in my head, it was as if I was in a trance-like state. In life sometimes you do get that one moment to make something happen and if you don't take the opportunity then you may never get that shot again. I was steadily getting more pumped up as the DVD and the song went on and I could feel the adrenaline rushing through every pore of my body. By the time the buzzer sounded in the changing room, to get us out for kick off, I had never been more pumped up in my entire life. Nothing had ever touched or spoken to me so strongly and I was ready to put everything I had out on the pitch.

Yet despite being psyched up, and playing well, we went a goal down. We threw the kitchen sink at them to try to equalise but with only two minutes remaining it looked as if it wasn't going to be our night and we were set to crash out of the promotion chase yet again. However, those final two minutes would become the most cherished of my career.

I remember that around the 89-minute mark, I picked up the ball on the right wing and whipped in a great cross. Marc Goodfellow rose high above one of their defenders and headed the ball down into the bottom left hand corner of the goal. Ashton Gate went bonkers, it was 1–1, our season was still alive and momentum was with us as we were set for extra time. However, there was still more drama to come.

In the final seconds of the 90 minutes the ball was flicked on to me about 25 yards from goal on the left hand side of the pitch. I took a touch into the penalty area and was about to pull the trigger when I saw a Hartlepool player ready to fling himself in the way. As he jumped in I disguised the shot with my left foot and instead pulled the ball across my body. The Hartlepool player had committed himself and he slid out of my way. I was now about six yards from goal, on an angle, and with the goalkeeper running out towards me. With my foot ready to pull the trigger I noticed that another defender was galloping up right behind me trying to make a last ditch tackle. Just as the defender went through the back of me I slotted the ball through the keeper's legs. As I fell to the ground I could see the ball cross the line and hit the back of the net, cue 19,000 Bristolians going absolutely mental. Sheer pandemonium broke out in the stands.

When the ball went in, I completely lost my head, I started running and screaming to myself. My teammates tried to grab hold of me but I pushed them off and kept running. I felt like I was going to explode. Finally I dived into the corner and everyone jumped on top of me. The boys screamed all sorts into my ear and I was yelling incoherently. Even when everyone finally got off me I lay sprawled on the grass screaming to myself. The season had been a disaster but I had stepped up when it mattered most.

No matter how much drink I might have got through it never came anywhere near to providing me with the buzz that scoring that goal did. That rush after the ball went in must have only lasted for 30 seconds but it was the biggest rush I have had, or am ever likely to have. My head and heart were throbbing with emotion. I had scored the winning goal, in the last minute of the play off semi-final, to take us to the final, which was going to be played in the Millennium Stadium in my home city.

Seconds after my goal the referee blew the final whistle and the fans invaded the pitch. I had never seen so many happy faces run to embrace me. Even when I had some rough patches during that season the fans had stood by me and I was made up that I had delivered when it mattered most. The fans lifted me up on their shoulders and carried me around the pitch like a conquering hero. I'd dreamt about moments like those ever since I had first kicked a ball; I'd pictured myself scoring an important winning goal, the fans chanting my name, and carrying me around the pitch on their shoulders. I can't thank the Bristol fans enough for making my dreams come true.

When I finally left the pitch, and made my way down the tunnel, I was besieged by reporters wanting to interview me. Over the last few months I had been the forgotten man and now all of a sudden I was the centre of attention, and it felt fantastic. During an interview with Sky in the changing room I could barely hear anything as all the boys were going ballistic behind me. They even poured a jug of water over my head whilst I was speaking.

It's weird as even though that was, without a doubt, the finest moment of my career, I haven't been able to watch the footage of it on YouTube until recently. Every time I have tried to watch it the emotion of it all is too much for me to handle. Whenever I see Bristol City fans, all they ever talk to me about is that goal. I'm happy that I'm remembered for doing something like that.

That night though I must have watched those final two minutes a hundred times. My friend, and former Cardiff City player, Tony Bird, had been at Ashton Gate to watch me play so after the game we went back to my house in Cardiff and watched it over and over. Janine was with us and we all had some drinks to celebrate. Yet when everyone else had gone to bed I was still up by myself in the early hours watching the footage and getting through as many cans of Stella as possible.

With over a week to prepare for the final against Brighton at the Millennium Stadium, the hype surrounding the game seemed to reach fever pitch. Everyone was talking about my semi-final goal and the fact that I would be a Cardiff boy playing in my home city. It seemed to be destiny that I would fire us into the Championship. I lost count of how many people truly believed that this was going to happen.

Danny Wilson was keen to keep our pre-match preparation similar to our preparation for the play off semis as I think he thought that if we changed anything at that stage then it could make us nervous on the big day. We didn't even have special suits made as most clubs do for finals; we had to wear our club tracksuit.

Another thing we kept the same was watching the Al Pacino/Eminem DVD again. It was strange, as I didn't get the same buzz watching it for a second time. Don't get me wrong, it was still powerful but it didn't produce the same super human feeling I got when I first saw it. Looking back we probably should have done something a bit different, especially considering it was the final.

Walking out into the Millennium Stadium on such a big occasion was an emotional experience for me. A few years previously I had been bombed out by Cardiff City and now I was here, ready to shove the doubters' words right down their throats, if they thought I hadn't done so already.

But in the end the day turned into a complete nightmare. My old Cardiff teammate, Charlie Oatway, was playing for Brighton and I remember the first time I got the ball he smashed me and as we were on the floor he pinched my arm so hard I had a bruise there for weeks. 'Charl, what you doing?' I asked.

'Fuck off you little twat,' was his charming reply. Off the field I was good mates with Charlie, and had a lot of time for him, but out there in the play off final our friendship was paused for 90 minutes.

The team didn't get going and I had a particularly poor game. It was billed as being my day but I didn't perform. We ended up losing the game 1–0 and once more we had failed to get promotion for the third successive year in my time at the club. It was heartbreaking; the atmosphere in the changing room was the worst I have ever experienced in football. There were tears, screams and tantrums, no one could believe that we had failed again.

After the game the club had organised a party for us back in Bristol so we all had to travel on the coach from Cardiff together. I didn't want to go, I wanted to be left by myself so that I could wallow in my own misery with an ocean of alcohol. I even asked Frank Barlow if I could stay in Cardiff but he said, 'We win and lose together' so I had no option.

The night was so depressing, all the lads were distraught and we couldn't quite believe we hadn't got promoted. Everything seemed in place, yet once again we hadn't quite done it. I felt sorry for Danny Wilson, even though I had come good in the last 10 games of the season, as I felt guilty about all those games I turned up pissed or hungover. In an effort to make amends I bought Danny a bottle of champagne and we tried to smooth things over. Again I was so wasted I can't quite recall what was said but I think the general gist of it was how we all needed to regroup and do everything that we could to get promoted the following season. I liked Danny; I had a lot of time for him as a manager, and as a man, so I was looking forward to playing for him again the next year when I hoped I would finally savour a promotion party but unfortunately it was not to be.

11

MOVING ON

Danny's contract was up that summer, but we all fully expected it to be renewed, so I was stunned when I heard that it wasn't. I was even more shocked when I heard that my friend and teammate, Brian Tinnion, had been appointed in his place.

Brian was a legend at Bristol City. He joined the club in 1993 and had made over 450 appearances during his time as a Robin. There is no getting away from the fact that as a player he had been top notch with a dream of a left foot, yet this was going to be his first managerial appointment and I wasn't altogether sure it was a good move for him, or for the club. I thought they would have been better sticking with Danny.

It wasn't that I was completely disappointed with Brian's appointment at the time though, he was a friend and I was sure that he rated me as a player. As teammates we got on well, we had gone to the same places on holiday and played cards together. If I had managed to sneak a few cans of lager on the team coach, and was in the process of drinking them, he would warn me when the Gaffer was on his way up, so I had a lot of time for him as a bloke.

At the time my contract with Bristol City only had one more year left to run, and I was desperate for it to be renewed, so that I could continue to afford my drinking habit. By this point I was in deep financial shit. I hid most of my financial issues from Janine but I was spending way more than I was earning and if my contract wasn't renewed then I could have been facing disaster. With Brian in charge I was confident that he would dig me out of my hole and offer me a few more years on at least the same money.

When I reported back for pre-season training I approached Brian about getting a new deal, but he didn't really seem that interested. He told me that I would have to wait a few months before he would discuss it and didn't give me a reason. I was furious! Not only with Brian, but also because my financial future was going to face an uncertain couple of months. Not that the lack of new contract talks stopped me drinking or spending money on extravagant things that I didn't really need.

Early on it became clear to the old guard at Bristol that Brian was going to clean the decks and introduce some of the youngsters into the team such as Leroy Lita and Liam Rosenoir. Both lads were great prospects but the old boys were desperate to make amends for missing out on promotion the previous season. Brian put a few noses out of joint and it certainly didn't make for a happy ship.

I was one of those who spent a lot of time on the sidelines, as Brian seemed determined to freeze me out. To be honest I found it all a bit surprising. Yes, I was a raging alcoholic, but Brian didn't know that. In the last 10 games of the previous season I had shown that I could be a match winner and I felt I deserved more of a chance. As a friend Brian had always 'bigged' me up but now, a few months later, his attitude towards me had changed.

Of course I understood that as a manager he could not be as close to us all like when he had been a teammate, but I didn't agree with the way he went about things. The disharmony in the team was reflected in the disappointing results Bristol achieved under Brian. It was also clear that the job was too big for him at that stage of his career. Bristol is a big club, especially in a division like League One, and the standards we had come to expect in training and preparation were sadly lacking in comparison to what they had been under Danny Wilson.

Brian and me had been friends, but as a manager I lost a lot of respect for him. I think he treated me poorly. When I was out of the side at the start of the season he kept saying I would get my chance, and that we would soon discuss a new deal, but nothing happened. He seemed to be buttering me up to avoid a confrontation. If he had a problem with my drinking, attitude, performances in games or training then he should have brought it up, but he didn't. I didn't know what I had done wrong or how to rectify the situation.

The fact that Brian made it clear, by continually not picking me, that I didn't have a future at Bristol spurred on my alcohol consumption. I would think to myself, I'm not going to play so I may as well get shit faced. It was not really the attitude to have when trying to earn a new contract but it was obvious that wasn't going to happen anyway.

On 22 September 2004 we played Everton at

Ashton Gate in the League Cup. It was the first, and only, time in my career that I played a Premier League team and I definitely learnt a thing or two. For once I started the game and we performed well on the night despite eventually losing 3–2 in extra time.

I was up against Joseph Yobo, the Everton centre-back, and I soon learned about the difference in standard of players in League One and the Premiership. It's not just their touch or reading of the game that makes them elite players, they are all unbelievable athletes. Yobo was big, strong and fast; he was virtually impossible to out-think or get past through brute strength or speed. Considering I reeked of booze after another bender I didn't play too badly but what chance did I have against a player of that calibre when I hadn't even prepared properly?

After the game I rushed into the players' bar, so I could grab my customary after-match pint, when I saw Swindon manager, Andy King, in the room smoking his trademark cigar. The last time I had seen Andy King was during a game at the County Ground, when I had not only scored against Swindon, but also had kicked Brian Howard so hard that it sparked a huge fight which ended up with Andy and me going toe to toe and threatening to knock each other out.

Despite that encounter I had a lot of time for Kingy and as I approached the bar he said, cigar still firmly clamped between his lips, 'What's the story with you here then?'

'I haven't got a clue,' I honestly replied, 'Brian doesn't seem to want me around.'

Kingy looked bemused. The following day I heard from my agent that he'd been in touch and wanted me to join Swindon.

A move to Swindon definitely appealed to me. They were not only a good side in League One, who had also reached the play off semi-finals the previous season, but I could also continue to commute from my home in Cardiff. I had always liked Andy King as well, he was a player's manager, one of the lads, and I thought he could get the best out of me. It was also a nice feeling to be wanted again.

The only slight stumbling block was that Swindon and Bristol were fierce rivals and I never liked the thought of upsetting the fans. Yet I had already played for Bristol as a Cardiff boy and that had worked out so I was sure that things would be fine once the dust had settled. At the end of the day, playing football was my livelihood as well and it had been made clear that my days at Bristol were numbered. Any decent club willing to pay me a salary, and play me, had to be seriously considered, regardless of who they were.

The deal was thrashed out over the next few days, without much hesitation from Bristol I might add. I was worried that I may have a problem with my medical, due to the amount I had been drinking, but it was a joke. I had a light jog on a running machine, the doctor had a brief look at my knee and then that was it; I had passed and I was officially a Swindon Town player.

In all honesty, whilst I was pleased to move to Swindon, and to play for Andy King, in hindsight it was probably the worst move I could have made. Not long after signing it became clear that as long as players did the business in games it didn't matter to Kingy how they looked after themselves, they would play. As soon as I worked that out I quite happily abused the system, I couldn't believe my luck. I remember thinking to myself, 'Christian, you've had a right result here'.

Whilst I had hardly been a model pro at Bristol in the back of my mind I knew that if I didn't keep up a certain minimum standard in training then I would get nowhere near the squad. At Swindon I literally did nothing; I was an absolute disgrace and would turn up in all sorts of states.

It says a lot about my frame of mind at this time that I ordered a brand new Audi A4 and had the glove box converted into a fridge so I could store cans of Stella in it. On my way to training I chugged down a few cans and then when we were finished I had a nice cold Stella waiting for me to enjoy on the way back home. We would finish training in Swindon at 12.00pm and by 1.00pm I would already be back in Cardiff chucking pints down my neck.

My diet and fitness also went completely out of the window and as a result I started to put weight on. When we were weighed at the club, Dick the physio stood at the side and we had to call out our weight so that he could record it. I wouldn't even look at the scales, I merely called out, 'Twelve and a half stone!' and no one said a thing.

Despite my abysmal training regime, I somehow managed to play quite well at times and Kingy happily kept selecting me. I made myself a fan's favourite on my debut at the County Ground when I scored the winner against Oldham. I then swiftly followed up that goal with strikes against Barnsley, Sheffield Wednesday and Hull. As a player I knew that I could be inconsistent, and infuriate fans at times, but when I was on song I could excite them and fans always like players who can get them out of their seats. Soon the Swindon fans 'forgave' me for having played for their rivals, Bristol City, and started singing, 'Oh Christian Roberts! He used to play for City but he's alright now!' In some games I sang along as I was playing!

Shortly after I arrived at Swindon, the club organised a team-bonding day out at the races and this is where I really learnt how much I could get away with under Kingy. Matthew Heywood, Alan Reeves, Brian Howard, Andy Guirney, Andy King, Mick Harford and me spent our time there in a tent playing cards and getting wrecked. By the time evening arrived Peter Reid joined us and the drinks and banter were flowing. We all started getting a bit boisterous, no one more so than Kingy, who was in the middle of all of the mischief.

It must have been obvious to him that I was a drinker as he challenged me to a drinking competition to see who could down their pint of Caffrey's through a straw the fastest. Fair play to him, he absolutely killed me, but then I issued a challenge to see who could down their drink the quickest. I was in a different league when it came to downing a pint, I could pour it down my throat as quick as you could pour it on the floor. In fact, some people thought I could do it even quicker than that, I seemed to be able to suck it straight out of the glass. Kingy stood no chance and after that he had to go to bed. However, we all continued drinking long into the night and had a hell of a session.

On Boxing Day 2004 I injured my groin in a 2–0 win away to Peterborough and it turned out that I had a hernia and would need surgery to repair it. That injury kick-started a chain of events that took my drinking to a new low.

A few days after the Peterborough game Janine, the kids and me went to a party at our friends, Kevin and Nicky's, house. During the party I pretty much ignored my family and concentrated on drinking the house dry of alcohol. Janine was obviously pissed off, she approached me and angrily said, 'I'm going to take the kids home. Are you coming?' There was no way I was going with them, I hadn't even begun to satisfy my thirst yet and there was still plenty of free booze on offer. She took off with the kids and left me to do a number on myself.

For some reason, once Janine and the kids were gone, I began to think about how they always got in the way of my drinking and that perhaps I would be better off without them. I stayed the night on Kevin and Nicky's settee and I realised that I didn't want to go back home, all I wanted to do was drink non-stop without being made to feel guilty about it. With that in mind I decided to rent myself a little place, where I could drink with no distractions, and walked out on my family.

As I was waiting for an operation on my groin injury I didn't have to play or train, and now I had my own place, nothing prevented me from day after day of the most ridiculous drinking. For the rest of December, and early January, I must have been drinking 20 pints of Stella a day and that doesn't count all the shorts and shots I would fit in as well.

I finally had my hernia operation on the morning of Friday 14 January 2005 and later that day my brother picked me up from the hospital and drove me to my

*Training hard after my spell
in the Sporting Chance clinic*

Textbook technique

*Celebrating a goal whilst captain of Swindon Town as we stormed to the top of the
league*

In my element, running with the ball, whilst with Swindon Town

Trying to forget about the pain in my knee whilst in pre-season training for Swindon in Austria

He shoots....

He scores ...

Ethan sporting his dad's shirt

Me and some of the kids from Llanrumney on a day trip to Wembley

My boys chillin'

With my girlfriend Ceri Prince

Back in action after rehab

© Chris Adams, Swindon Town

With great friend and former manager, Chelsea legend, Gus Poyet, at my Swindon Town testimonial

Having the time of my life. Taking a coaching session for my company, Total Technique

The boys on holiday

Janine and the boys

*This is what makes it all worthwhile,
putting a smile on the faces of kids in
my community!*

Ethan and Ewan scrub up well!

Me with the man I admire more than any other, my father!

new rented home. He thought I was going inside to recuperate, but I had other plans. Once he had gone I limped down to my local pub, The Village Inn, and spent the rest of the weekend guzzling drinks like a maniac.

When I woke up on Monday morning I realised something was drastically wrong, there was a bubble the size of a small football coming out of my groin. I had to go back to the hospital and they drained litre after litre of fluid from the bubble and advised me that to stop it happening again, I needed to rest in bed. No chance, I was back in the pub that afternoon drinking myself into oblivion.

My first game back from injury was against Luton on 12 March 2005 but from then until May I entered the darkest period yet of my alcohol addiction. It was no wonder that I didn't score a goal in that period as my fitness completely went out of the window.

One game that I think was in this period was when we lost 2–1 to Walsall at home. Paul Merson, the former Arsenal and England legend, was player-manager of Walsall and he was playing right wing whilst I was on the left so we were up against each other. Paul has had well publicised drink, drugs and gambling problems during his career and I was, of course, struggling with my own demons. I don't know if Paul had had a few drinks before the game but he seemed a bit off it, and one thing was certain, I was still rat assed from a session the previous night. We were both struggling so Paul offered me a deal, 'Tell you what, let's take it easy against each other in this game and hopefully we will both look okay'. It sounded good to me so we carried on the game doing just that, it was a joke. Did I care? Did I fuck! I was playing so I was getting my appearance money and as long as I could afford my drink then I was happy.

The only problem was that I was really struggling financially, despite getting a three-year contract at Swindon, as I had spent every single penny that I owned on alcohol. I even switched from Stella to cider, as it was cheaper, yet I still couldn't afford to maintain my habit. One week I pawned my Rolex watch on a Friday but by the Monday I had spent every penny that I received for it on booze. Cheques I wrote were bouncing left right and centre and I was receiving letters threatening to take me to court if I didn't settle my bills.

It got so bad that one month I told Janine that Swindon hadn't paid me so I couldn't give her any money for her and the kids. I was borrowing money from all over the place, not only from banks and credit companies, but also from friends and family. I would say I had forgotten my bank card, and needed £50 to put petrol in my car, and my brother would give it to me but that would go straight on alcohol. Slowly but surely I was digging myself deeper into the abyss and just about keeping my head above water.

By the end of the season I was beginning to feel lonely drinking by myself and started to regret walking out on my family. Janine and me decided to go on a family holiday to Dubai together where we could talk and see if there was any way that we could sort things out between us. When we were there Janine said that if things were going to work then I needed to address my drinking issues. I promised that I would stop drinking on weekdays and would only drink on weekends from now on and she was happy with that.

When we returned, I tried to keep my promise and for that first week I didn't touch any alcohol but it was hell. It was the hardest week of my life; I was bitter, twisted and pure evil to be around. If the kids so much as spoke I would bite their heads off and it soon became clear to me that I couldn't survive without alcohol in my system. After five days of sobriety I was back on it. Yet, amazingly, I justified to myself that it was obvious I didn't have a problem as I could go five days without a drink.

By the second week I was back on the booze harder than ever but trying to hide it as best I could so that Janine couldn't find out. It's funny, I had been drinking alcohol for so long that my personality when I was drunk became me. Therefore whenever I was drunk no one thought anything of it, they thought I was being myself. Alcohol had completely taken me over and I had turned into a monster.

12

THE ABYSS

During pre-season in 2005 I began to realise that drink was having an adverse affect on my health. Whilst training I was struggling to breathe and generally felt like shit. After one session I remember I told my teammate Gareth Whalley, semi-jokingly, 'I don't feel right Gaz. I can see myself going in for treatment this year'. We both laughed but deep down inside I felt that things were getting out of hand.

By September 2005 I was in one hell of a mess, I realised that I couldn't stand not being able to drink 24/7 and I walked out on my family again. It was the height of selfishness but in my head I didn't see a problem with it. Drink was the number one priority in my life and my wife and kids were getting in the way of that. Any alcoholic will tell you that drink comes above absolutely everything. This time my drinking went out of the stratosphere, from September 05 to January 06 I did the hardest, sickest, drinking of my life. If I wasn't training or playing then I had a drink in my hand.

After leaving my family I moved in with Pops, but in the five months that I lived with him I probably spent only two nights in his house as I would prefer to sleep anywhere I didn't have to hide my alcohol consumption. As is the case with most addicts, I started mixing with the wrong crowd and borrowing money off dodgy people to feed my addiction. It was pure day-to-day survival where I was trying to scrape together enough pennies to be able to afford the amount of alcohol my body demanded. I have lost count of the amount of times that I woke up, after a night out, in a crack den, with people shooting up heroin around me and then stumbled into my car steaming to drive to training.

One day I was driving back to Cardiff, after I had finished training in Swindon, and I felt massively depressed. My finances were in meltdown and I was feeling low. My mood wasn't helped when Janine called and we ended up having a huge blow out. As I was crossing the Severn Bridge I pulled over to the side, got out of my car and peered over the edge. I had enough of it all and I thought, 'If I jump now will anyone even miss me?' My mind and body was at breaking point and rather than address my problems, jumping seemed the easiest option. I looked over the edge and started to climb over the barrier, fully intending to throw myself off the bridge. As I climbed over the barrier I suddenly snapped out of my self pity, 'What the fuck am I doing?' I thought.

I instantly returned to the car and cried my eyes out. I was emotionally and financially shot, and I still didn't know what I could do to get myself together but at least I realised that jumping off a bridge wasn't the answer. The only thing that I could think of to help my situation was drink, so I drove straight to the pub and went on another huge session. That ended up pouring more fuel onto the fire.

Not only was my personal life a shambles, but life on the football pitch was also becoming a disaster. Our start to the 2005–06 season had been very disappointing as we registered just two wins in our first 14 games and we were rock bottom of the league. Unsurprisingly, in September 2005, the board lost patience and Andy King was sacked after we lost five games in a row. Iffy Onoura was appointed as the new manager and it turned out to be the most important managerial appointment of my life.

Iffy was already at Swindon as a youth development officer and he was well liked by the players and the staff. It was his first managerial appointment, and we were a club in crisis, so it was a gamble by the board but I'm so glad that they took that risk as otherwise my life could have turned out differently.

Even with a new manager to impress, and with a new regime where we were expected to train hard, I still didn't sort myself out. The drinking had become so hardcore that I was pissing and spitting up blood on a regular basis. Every drink that I had felt like someone was poking searing hot barbed wire around inside me, it had long ceased to be a pleasant experience. When I went into the pub I had to order two pints as the first pint always made me sick after a few sips, and I would throw up in the glass. I needed the second pint next to me as I knew that one would be more enjoyable. The drink was ripping my body to shreds but it still didn't stop me. There is no doubt that I was going to keep drinking until I dropped dead.

I had always taken pride in my appearance but now I didn't care. The time it took me to dress and wash would be time that I could spend drinking so I basically stopped bothering. I wore the same tracksuit for weeks at a time and went two months without shaving at one point. I looked and acted like a wino, yet I was still a highly paid professional footballer.

My appearances on the pitch steadily started to suffer and I found myself out of the side. Again I thought I was being victimised and couldn't understand how I could be left out. Everything in my personal and professional life was rapidly falling apart and it was all going to come to a head if I carried on drinking.

For the first time, in November 2005, I suddenly began to realise that I had a serious drink problem that needed addressing. I can even remember the exact moment when I thought to myself that I needed help. During this time the legendary footballer, George Best, was close to death, due to liver failure, after his own highly publicised battle with alcohol. I remember sitting in the pub reading the paper when I saw a picture of George in his hospital bed, with his son Calum standing next to him. George looked horrendous, he was bright yellow and nothing but skin and bone. I kept looking at that picture thinking, 'That could be me'. Seeing George's son, Calum, stood next to his sick father also had a profound effect on me and I vowed that I would not put my kids through the same ordeal.

The light had finally been switched on in my head, I realised that I had some sort of problem but I didn't immediately know what to do about it. For the next few weeks I carried on drinking, yet in the back of my mind I was starting to think about whether I needed some sort of treatment. I couldn't face rehab right away but every time that I passed blood it was a stark reminder that something was wrong. Thankfully Iffy Onoura intervened and probably saved my life.

During training, the day before our game against Rotherham, Iffy pulled me aside and told me that I would be on the bench, I went berserk. In the previous game we had lost 3–0 to Barnsley, but I felt that I hadn't played too badly and that others should have been dropped before me. In all honesty, because of the state that I was in by now due to booze, I probably had not been playing or training well for a while. Another factor in my tantrum was that if I was on the bench I would miss out on some much needed appearance money. Despite my hissy fit I sat out the game and the lads came away with a 1–0 victory.

A couple of days after the Rotherham game, I arrived in Swindon for training and Iffy called me into his office. I had a massive beard and my tracksuit must have stunk as it hadn't been washed in a week. Iffy looked me up and down and said, 'Everything okay?'

'Yeah,' I replied, lying through my backside, 'all's good.' He then mentioned something about the amount I was drinking. It was the first time that anyone in football had approached me about it. At first I tried to cover up and told him with a straight face, 'I like a beer but it's not as if it's a problem'.

Iffy didn't look convinced; he said, 'Look Chris, I'm going to do you a favour. I'm going to give you the next week off to have a look at yourself'. I didn't immediately grasp what he was on about, and I didn't want to argue as I thought that I could get some serious drinking done in that time off.

As I walked out of the office, and headed towards the dressing room, it suddenly struck me. This was the moment that I had to make a choice. I either sought help now or I drank myself to death. Immediately I turned back, walked into Iffy's office and blurted out, 'Iffy, I need help'.

Iffy had recognised that I had some serious issues but he didn't want to drag me off to rehab if I wasn't prepared to admit I had a problem. He knew that if he did then I would explode, so his subtle approach was a masterstroke and it worked.

He phoned Peter Kay, the Chief Executive of the Sporting Chance Clinic, and explained that I needed to see him. The Sporting Chance Clinic was set up by former England captain, Tony Adams, after his own battle with alcohol addiction and it has a fantastic reputation for helping footballers overcome their addictions.

I had spoken to Peter over a year earlier when I toyed with the idea of seeking help but I had never followed through with it. Iffy put me on the phone to Peter and the first thing he said to me was, 'I've been waiting all year for you to call'. We arranged a time for me to meet with him, and his team, within the next couple of weeks and that was that, I had taken the first inch towards sorting my life out.

When I got off the phone Iffy reassured me that he and the club would stand by me. That meant a lot as without Iffy Onoura and Swindon Town's support it would have made things impossible and I doubt whether I would have sought help. It was agreed that I would go down to the Sporting Chance Clinic for an assessment before enrolling for full time treatment.

One of the hardest things I had to do was tell Pops that I was going to seek treatment. I don't think he fully realised the extent of my drinking as I had always hidden it from him so it came as a bit of a shock. However, when I opened up to him he was supportive as he had dealt with my Mum's drinking issues for years. She had never sought treatment and I think he admired me for giving it a go. I must have looked like a down and out when I told him, though, as Pops suggested that I have a haircut and shave before I went for my assessment at Sporting Chance. Unbelievably I didn't have a penny to my name despite earning around 40 times what my old man did. He gave me some money for a haircut and for once I felt too guilty to spend it on drink. It was a real low.

13

GIVING LIFE
A CHANCE

One month after my telephone conversation with Peter Kay I drove down to the Sporting Chance Clinic in Forestmere, Hampshire for an assessment. As I drove there I felt proud that I was giving myself a chance. I didn't really know what to expect but I had the impression that I would be advised to have a week's worth of treatment and then I would be able to control my drinking. At no point did I think I was going to have to stop drinking completely and if I had thought that, I would have probably had second thoughts about going.

Upon arriving at the clinic I couldn't believe how isolated the place was. It was literally just two small cottages in the middle of the countryside, it was eerily quiet and there weren't any other villages around for miles. The clinic isn't like one of those celebrity treatment centres like The Priory which is open 24/7, Sporting Chance only opens when it has patients. It was a beautiful setting though and I could see that it would be peaceful enough to enable me to focus on sorting out my issues.

When I walked into one of the cottages I met Peter Kay, the Chief Executive, Julian Keeling, the Senior

Therapist, and James West, the Clinical Director. All three have had battles with addiction and are highly respected in their fields.

Peter is a Michelin-starred chef but had such a chronic alcohol addiction that he suffered two cardiac arrests and was in a coma for 21 days.

Julian was a successful journalist but became addicted to drugs and alcohol. After receiving help in 1997 he re-trained to become a counsellor so that he could pass his expertise onto other addicts.

James is from a music background but changed his career after becoming addicted to drugs and alcohol and being sent to jail for six years for drug related offences. On his release he re-trained and is now an expert psychotherapist.

All three guys were not only switched on, but also looked successful and happy. It was motivating to see how they had overcome their own addictions to go on and live a life without the need for drugs and alcohol. Even though they were former addicts themselves, I still wasn't quite ready to open up to them. I remember thinking that I needed to convince them that my problems weren't that bad and that maybe I didn't even need any treatment.

After we all had an initial discussion, Peter suggested I go with Julian to the cottage next door where we could speak a bit more about my drinking. During our discussion I lied to Julian's face as I told him that I had a few beers a day but not much more than that. I was telling him what I thought he wanted to hear so that at the end of our session he could tell me that I didn't have a problem.

I was with Julian for around two hours, and he was

probing into all areas of my life trying to get to the bottom of how bad my addiction was, but I wouldn't let him below the surface. When we were done we went back to the cottage next door, where Peter and James were waiting for us, and I thought I had convinced Julian that I would need minimal treatment at most.

As we walked into the cottage Peter said to Julian, 'So how did he do?'

'He's one of us,' Julian replied.

'What the hell does that mean?' I thought. I couldn't believe that he had seen through my act. From that day on I knew that I couldn't lie to those guys, they were way too clever for that.

We all sat back down and Peter advised me that I needed to go on their 28-day residential programme in order to sort out my issues. I was stunned; I thought that I would only need a week of treatment at the most. It was now clear that the purpose of going for treatment was so I would never be able to have a drink again and that scared me. I still wasn't convinced that I wanted to stop drinking altogether and in the back of my mind I was already thinking that I would still be able to have the occasional drink when I got out. To be honest I didn't really know if I could handle getting completely sober.

After the assessment it was agreed that I would go back home for a few weeks before beginning treatment. However, I wouldn't be returning to football just yet as my head was all over the place so Iffy let me train whilst I sorted myself out. He told me not to worry about the football, but to concentrate on becoming a human being again.

Iffy's support didn't stop me feeling guilty though. The team was fighting relegation and he could have done with me in the squad but he put my well being ahead of his ambition as a manager. After that season I only had one more year left on my contract and I vowed that I would play out that year and if I deserved a new deal at the end of it then it would be for football reasons and not because someone was doing me a favour. I owed it to Iffy, and to myself, to become a proper professional footballer again and to try to play to my potential.

I think the club wanted to see how bad my situation was as the doctor, John Ellerman, started to take a lot more interest in me. At the start of this book I told you he found that my liver score was 66 when a healthy adult's score should be 26. When he asked me how many drinks I had a day I told him, 'Just the 2 or 3', when in fact I would drink that amount within the first 15 minutes of a session. I wasn't ready to tell everyone what was actually going on, but the test results showed that I was telling bare faced lies. I was still trying to be a smart ass so that people wouldn't find out the full extent of my problems. My lies were ridiculous, I was getting so used to lying by now that sometimes I believed what I was saying, no matter how far-fetched.

Those few weeks before I checked in for treatment were strange. On the one hand I was trying to get sober, yet on the other I was still drinking as much as before. Some days I would scale it down a bit, but other days I would drink the bar dry. At times I tried to see if I could control my drinking by myself but it was obvious that I couldn't without seeking help.

Before I went into treatment I decided to inform the

media about my situation. Whilst I didn't yet admit that I was an alcoholic, as I hadn't admitted that to myself at that point, I did confirm that I was seeking treatment for some issues. I know of some instances where footballers have sought treatment, and hid behind a smokescreen by saying that they are injured but I didn't want to do that. I always felt that it was important to be honest with the media and told the reporters that if they had a story they could contact me and I would give them a statement. That policy usually stood me in good stead throughout my career and perhaps stopped me getting bad press when I no doubt deserved it.

A few days before I was due to check in at the clinic I received a brochure outlining what I could expect during my stay there. It all sounded a bit daunting but I was ready to give it a go. The brochure said that I should not drink alcohol for 72 hours before entering the facility and I was expected to report at the clinic at 9.00am on 16 January 2006.

Despite being warned that I could not drink 72 hours before treatment, I miscalculated and thought that I could have my last drink at 11.00pm Friday 13 January 2006 when in fact it should have been 11.00am that morning. I remember I was at The Village Inn and at 10.45pm I still had half my pint left and I decided to leave it. I didn't need to take my drinking right up to what I thought the deadline was, I was going to be stronger than that. Walking out of the pub, still relatively sober, knowing I had a weekend of no drinking ahead of me was hard but I was determined to see it through. Friday 13th is unlucky for some but it turned out to be the date of my last drink so I will always associate that date with a turning point in my life.

With my weekend a designated no drinking zone I wanted to be alone as I knew I would be murder to be around. Janine bought me some non-alcoholic lager as she thought that may help me psychologically, but I had one sip and threw the stuff away. Not only did it taste horrible but I thought, 'Why am I even tempting myself with "fake" lager?' I know what a Stella tastes like and drinking an inferior version made me crave the real stuff. I somehow managed to get through that weekend without touching a drop but it was hard work and at times I felt like climbing the walls.

At 7.00am on Monday morning I left Cardiff and made my way to Forest Mere to finally sort out my life. On the way I passed a lovely pub in a little village and for a split second I thought, 'Fuck it!' and was tempted to pull over and get hold of as much booze as possible. Somehow I resisted and when I finally pulled into the clinic at 8.45am, and handed over my keys and phone, I was relieved to have made it without falling victim to temptation.

When I arrived, Steve Rice, Arsenal legend Pat Rice's son, was already checking in. Steve was also at the clinic for alcohol abuse and he was busy saying goodbye to his family who had travelled with him. We were also expecting former Leeds United and Middlesbrough forward, Noel Whelan, to join us but as ever he was fashionably late. What a kid he was! I had heard about his legendary partying through the grapevine in the football world and he was a top man. As soon as I met both Steve and Noel I was grateful that we would be going through this experience together as they were great guys.

Once Noel arrived we were taken to the cottage

where we would be staying for the next 28 days. The cottage was relatively basic and was definitely not the luxurious establishment associated with professional footballers. The first room we saw had a double bed and an ensuite bathroom and Noel immediately bagged that one. The next room was spacious with two beds in, whilst the last remaining room was a box room with a single bed. I wanted the box room, I wasn't there for luxury; I was there to punish myself and get well and I thought that the box room would help me do that. Steve happily took the bigger room.

After we had thrown our stuff into our rooms, we had to meet all the staff in the opposite cottage at 9.20am so that Peter could explain how the programme would work.

Following the introductory meeting we were sent to Champney's Health Spa, a 10-minute walk down the road, so that we could undergo a medical. Steve was the first to be seen and both Noel and I were relieved. Steve was a normal working man, whilst Noel and I were professional footballers, so we counted on Steve weighing more than the two of us and therefore we were confident that we wouldn't get shown up. As Steve was in the room Noel said that he was usually 14% body fat whilst I said I was 12% and weighed around 12 stone 8 pounds.

When Steve finally came out he said that he was recorded at 18% body fat. Noel and I sniggered amongst ourselves and were relieved, as there was no way we would be anywhere near that amount. Noel was up next and when he came out he looked gutted, his body fat reading was 19%. Oh how I slaughtered him, I called him every name under the sun, but I wish I had kept my mouth shut.

After the doctor had done my reading I was sure the machine was broken. It said that I weighed 14 stone 10 pounds and I had a body fat percentage of 21%! I couldn't believe it. How had I put on so much weight without realising it, let alone been able to play professional football? When I looked at my body in the mirror I was shocked. A flabby mess had replaced my once toned physique, my beer gut was hanging over my shorts and I had man boobs. I was disgusted with myself.

With Noel and I feeling suicidal, Steve was in high spirits as we walked back to the clinic together. We returned to the cottages for a bit and I lay on the bed in my box room staring at the ceiling wondering how the hell I had let myself go so badly. I wasn't a professional athlete anymore; I was merely a sick human being.

A guy called Carl, who was in charge of fitness at Sporting Chance, put together a fitness and nutrition plan to help me get back in shape whilst I was in treatment. We did a lot of fitness work such as yoga, weights, swimming and running at Champneys, which was a lovely place. Whilst it was good to get fit again my priority was getting sober. I knew that if I could stay sober I would easily get back into shape as I would no longer be consuming thousands of calories a day in alcohol. It would also help that I wouldn't be training with a hangover so I could work off the fat. Staying away from alcohol was going to be my greatest challenge.

A typical day in the clinic went something like this: At 8.30am each morning we would take our prescribed vitamins and have breakfast together. Then, at 9.00am, we would have a group therapy session and when that was finished we would sit with our prescribed therapist for a one on one. My therapist was Julian and I immediately felt as if he understood my problems and could help me. I felt comfortable talking to him about my issues and for the first time ever I could tell somebody about my deepest and darkest secrets.

Once the individual therapy session was over we would do some fitness work at Champneys. After we had finished our fitness session we returned to our cottage where we read therapy books and wrote in a booklet about all the bad things that we had done because of alcohol. Try doing that for a month and still like yourself by the end of it. When, as an alcoholic, you analyse the bad things you have done due to drink it is a massive wake up call. I felt physically sick thinking about stuff like not wanting to take my son to the hospital when he had a broken leg so that I could go to the pub instead or throwing a pint glass at my wife. What had I become? Where was my father's son?

For the first two weeks of treatment you lose all sense of respect for yourself. I usually had a lot of arrogance and a bit of a swagger but that was hammered out of me. Part of the treatment is to break you down by forcing you to confront all the disgusting things you have done and then in the final two weeks they build you back up again so that when you leave the clinic you can be a respectful member of society.

Each evening we would attend an AA meeting somewhere in Hampshire and whilst I didn't initially want to go, I soon learnt just how vital those meetings would be in my recovery. In the introduction to this book I talked about the first meeting that I attended. Noel, Steve and I all went to the meetings together and it was weird to hear us all admit that we were alcoholics. It was the first time that I had admitted it to myself, or to anyone else, and from that moment on I knew that I could not touch another drop of alcohol. Finally I realised that I had a serious problem and AA was going to play a major part in helping me.

The structure of each AA meeting would usually be that each person quickly introduces themselves to the group. Then a person is designated as the Main Share, and they speak about their experiences as an addict and how they developed the strength to get well again. Most Main Share stories can be shocking and emotional and they certainly are a source of great inspiration to the other addicts in the room. When the Main Share has finished talking, the Chairman speaks for a bit and then that is usually the end of the session. After that first session, as we left, Julian put his arm around me as he could see how I had been affected by it all. When he did that I remember feeling real human warmth, he was my guardian angel.

After my first AA session we went back to the cottage, had a coffee and then retired to bed. My box room had no TV, and I had no music with me, so I lay in the dark in absolute silence and broke down. I spent half the night crying my eyes out. It suddenly hit me like a tidal wave what a mess I was making of my life. I had behaved disgustingly towards my family and I had treated the managers, players and fans of the football clubs I had played for with sheer contempt. My health was poor and my finances were in a desperate state. I was in danger of losing everything that was important to me due to alcohol and when I realised that, I was relieved that I had an opportunity to do something about it.

Those nights spent alone in that room were the hardest part of treatment. Of course speaking in therapy sessions was difficult but when I was by myself, thinking over all the mistakes I had made, it made me feel suicidal at times. Some nights I wouldn't sleep at all, I would sit in bed with tears streaming down my cheeks screaming into my pillow. As the alcohol completely left my system I spent some nights with my body shaking uncontrollably and covered in sweat as I suffered from withdrawal symptoms. It was tough but I had a new found resolve that this was my punishment and I was going to take it on the chin and emerge a new man.

Another difficult part of my time at the clinic was when I was allowed to speak to my two kids at home. On the phone to them I pretended that I was on holiday and that everything was fantastic. I didn't want them to hear the empty shell that I had become. When I heard their voices I hated myself for the crap I had put them through. I had suffered from a hard childhood but due to my career I could have provided my own children with everything that they could have wanted in a loving and caring home, yet I chose to make their lives as difficult as possible. After speaking to them I wanted to be alone for a bit so that I could compose myself. The reality of my situation was hitting home.

One of the most important things that I learnt in therapy was how you shouldn't compress things. The more you talk about the bad things that have happened in your life the more pressure you release. I always told everyone that I was fine and that everything was great. I was always the bubbly one but deep inside I was compressing all this grit in my stomach and it needed an outlet.

When I analysed some of the bad stuff that had happened to me, I realised that I should have sought counselling years ago. So many things had occurred which I had never really talked about such as growing up with my mother's drinking problems, the death of my good friend Claire Draine when I was 13, the two children that Janine and I lost and then getting bombed out of Cardiff City. I realise that a lot of great things had happened in my life as well but I had been carrying around all the other shit inside me for too long. I believe that alcoholism was in my genes and would have manifested itself no matter what happened but compressing all my feelings and emotions meant that when it did come to fruition it was a deadly combination.

Those therapy sessions were a tremendous help and if I could pinpoint one thing that really helped me get sober it was talking about the issues in my life. It seemed to lift a huge load off my mind and remove all the grit that I had been carrying around inside me.

Not everything was doom and gloom inside the clinic. One thing that I really enjoyed, which I didn't think I would, was horse riding. When I was first told that we would be working with horses I was less than impressed. Yet when we got going I absolutely loved it, I actually felt close to those animals, it was almost as if they could feel my pain and were helping me through it. In the end I couldn't wait for the days when we would work with them.

Slowly, but surely, all my barriers were removed. I was losing the ego and arrogance that I had carried around for so long and was becoming myself again. I felt like a new person and for the first time, in a long time, I was beginning to feel optimistic about the future.

When I finally left Sporting Chance on 9 February 2006 I knew that I could never drink again, and it honestly didn't bother me. The first thing I swore that I would do was to make amends to my family so I went straight back to my home in Cardiff and tried to rebuild the damage that I had caused. It was hard to begin with because Janine had become so used to me as a drunk that it was almost as if I was a new person. For a while I got the feeling that she was treading on eggshells as she thought that because I wasn't drinking I would be bad tempered but those days were now gone for good.

I vowed to become the best father that I could possibly be to my kids, like my Dad had been to me, so I started spending as much time as I could with my two boys and gradually we rebuilt the bonds that I had destroyed through drinking. It was rewarding doing things that made them happy rather than taking them down the pub so they could watch me drink.

Another thing I had to address immediately was the state of my finances. At one point I seriously considered declaring myself bankrupt but I discussed my issues with a debt management company and they helped to advise me how to sort everything out. It was tough but it needed to be done.

I did everything I could to prevent myself from being tempted to return to alcohol and it meant making some hard decisions. When I went into rehab I had a phone book with over 200 names in it. I deleted virtually all of them. Some people in there were a bad influence and others didn't understand how I now

167

needed to live my life. A lot of people thought I would still be okay to go up the pub and have a pint and they didn't realise that it wasn't an option for me anymore. For a while I was lonely but in time I made a new network of friends and rebuilt my ties with others.

I decided to get rid of everything and anything that reminded me of alcohol. Clothes and shoes were a big reminder and I threw away, or donated to charity, over 30 pairs of shoes and the majority of my clothes. Certain tracksuits that I had spent my life wearing up the pub were the first to go, as they contained nothing but bad memories for me.

An important thing that Julian told me when I was in Sporting Chance was that whilst I was an alcoholic, I was still a human being and I could do anything that I wanted as long as I didn't drink. Over time I built up the confidence to go into town and attend music nights and so on, and found that I could still enjoy myself without drinking. I would even buy my friends a round on the condition that I wouldn't handle the drinks myself, as I didn't want alcohol to spill on me, and I didn't want to feel a pint glass in my hand ever again. My aversion to alcohol was so great that I wouldn't even touch food with it in. All these routines were tiny inches towards keeping myself sober.

The one problem with addicts is that once you banish one addiction another one usually arrives in its place. In my case I became addicted to coffee, which is hardly a destructive force compared to alcohol, but it's not good when you're drinking it non-stop. Whilst I used to spend all my time sat in the pub I now spent all my time sat in Starbucks getting through 12 coffees in an afternoon. I suppose the caffeine became a substitute for alcohol but I also enjoyed being in a social gathering instead of being alone. When I told Julian about my issues with coffee he managed to wean me off the stuff, as he did with drink.

A key factor in keeping me sober is abiding by some of the 12 steps that I learnt in AA:

1. *Admit that you are powerless over alcohol and that your life had become unmanageable.*
2. *Come to believe that a Power greater than you could restore you to sanity.*
3. *Make a decision to turn your will and your life over to the care of God as you understand Him.*
4. *Make a searching and fearless moral inventory of yourself.*
5. *Admit to God, and to yourself, and to another human being the exact nature of your wrongs.*
6. *Be entirely ready to have God remove all these defects of character.*
7. *Humbly ask Him to remove my shortcomings.*
8. *Make a list of all persons we had harmed, and become willing to make amends to them all.*
9. *Make direct amends to such people wherever possible, except when to do so would injure them or others.*
10. *Continue to take personal inventory and when you are wrong promptly admit it.*
11. *Seek through prayer and meditation to improve your conscious contact with God as you understand Him, praying only for knowledge of His will for us and the power to carry that out.*

12. *Having had a spiritual awakening as the result of these steps, try to carry this message to alcoholics and to practise these principles in all our affairs.*

One step I immediately attempted was to make amends to all the people that I had let down due to drinking. One of those people was my old Bristol City boss, Danny Wilson, who was now manager of Hartlepool United. When Swindon played Hartlepool later that year I sought Danny out in his office and apologetically said to him, 'I'm sorry for letting you down at Bristol City. What can I do to help make up for it?'

Danny, the gentleman that he is, told me, 'Chris, it's not a problem. You just concentrate on keeping well'. That meant a lot to me and it lifted a weight off my shoulders. I will always have a lot of time for Danny Wilson, not only is he a fantastic manager, but he is also one of the nicest people in the game.

As you can tell from reading the steps, there is a lot of spirituality involved and before treatment I wouldn't have necessarily said that I was a spiritual person. In fact even when I left treatment I still didn't appreciate the significance that religion could play in my life, but as you will see later in the book, religion eventually provided me with great comfort and helped keep me sober.

With everything else in my life slowly getting back in order I desperately needed to get my career back on track. When I came out of rehab on the Thursday, Iffy contacted me and asked if I was ready to be part of the squad for the team's game at Bradford on Saturday. I wasn't sure whether I was ready but the club were desperately fighting relegation and I wanted to help Iffy out in any way that I could. I thought that playing football would take my mind off things and I was looking forward to getting amongst all the banter with the boys again so I told Iffy that if he needed me then I would play for him.

We travelled to Bradford on the Friday afternoon and that night I attended an AA meeting in my Swindon tracksuit. I got a few funny looks but I didn't care, I needed that AA meeting to keep me on the straight and narrow, regardless of where it was. It was the first Friday in years where I didn't touch a drop of alcohol before a game and it felt strange preparing for a game like a professional should.

I was on the bench the next day and as I was warming up Steve Claridge started to stretch next to me on the sideline. As we were stretching our groins he jokingly said, 'Don't worry about rehab. We've all been there'. I laughed and we had a bit of a joke but it wasn't until later that I learnt that Steve had himself fought a battle against gambling addiction.

With about 20 minutes remaining Iffy sent me on and whilst I was keen to make an impression it was surprising just how much my time in rehab had taken out of me. I didn't have anything in my legs but I ran my guts out and the team still gained a valuable point in a 1–1 draw. Iffy Onoura told the media after the game: 'I have said since I took over that this is about building a family atmosphere. So, instinctively, when Christian had a problem the thinking was that we need to look after one of our family members. Obviously I first had to check that the support was there from the club, and they told me to go ahead and manage it how I saw fit. It's like a pride of lions and to see Christian come back, it was really heart warming. The lads aren't daft, they joke and have a bit of banter, but deep down they have a lot of respect for what Christian has done and what he's been through. He has had to bare his soul and all the strides he has made have come from inside himself. Our regard and respect for him as a person is immense.'

On the Monday following the game, I called a press conference in Swindon where I was willing to discuss my time in rehab with the media. Peter Kay, from Sporting Chance, also came along to help me through it. It felt good to get everything off my chest publicly and to be fair to the media, they were all supportive. I told them:

After a few days in the clinic you start feeling things. Your mind and your ears and your eyes start to open up. You start to open doors and think about everything you have done. I feel a different person in every stretch of life now. Before, when I had a conversation with people, I'd only be interested in myself. Now I open my ears and eyes and when I talk to people I like to look at them, so I get their reaction. I have had some great conversations with a lot of people. My whole life is a new way of living now, and I'm enjoying it. It is a fantastic mental state when you can appreciate people again. That particularly means my family, who I thought I had lost, and my close friends.

It has been extremely hard for my family. I used to blame my wife when it was all about me. I cannot thank her enough for standing by me and giving me that chance. The best feeling I've had since getting out of the clinic was on Friday morning, waking up with my wife and kids. It made it all worthwhile. And then spending time with them on Sunday—going for a nice walk and having coffee, doing family things and spending quality time with my kids. I have a lot of making up to do with them but I've had the help and I can get through it now.

Friday night for example, I had been out of the clinic 24 hours and I went by myself to an AA meeting. And it was fantastic. Even though I was up in Bradford, the warmth was there as I walked in. It gives you the strength to keep going.

Today was probably my first sober training session in five years. And I really didn't want to get off the pitch because it was lovely.

My next match was my first game at the County Ground since I had left rehab and ironically it was against Rotherham, the team I had been dropped against just before I went into treatment. I will always cherish the crowd's reaction to me that day, they were magnificent and I felt blessed to play in front of such understanding people.

Unfortunately we lost to Rotherham and then in my next game we lost to Colchester. Trying to play football and remain sober was taking its toll on me so I had to make the hardest decision of my career, I told Iffy that my head and my body weren't quite ready for professional football yet and I would have to sit the season out. I knew that if I played I wouldn't be doing myself, the club, the fans, the players or the staff justice. There was no doubt in my mind that I wasn't in a fit state to perform to the required standard and that the team had a better chance of staying up with me not in it.

For the next few months I needed to concentrate on remaining sober and thought that playing football would make that job harder. For the rest of the season I simply trained to build myself up for the following year when I was determined to make my mark.

Even without the pressure of playing football alcohol still taunted me everywhere that I went and it was becoming hard to resist. Seeing a beer advert on TV would be like watching porn, I would literally be like a pervert drooling at the screen. If someone was drinking a pint of beer near me I would be like a zombie watching them sip every gulp and I would have an urge to grab the closest beer and down it as quickly as possible.

The biggest test for a recovering alcoholic is when something bad happens in their life and they feel that they need the comfort of the bottle to get them through. A few months after rehab my house was burgled and my car was stolen. Not long after that my son Ethan broke his arm and had to stay in hospital to have an operation. I felt so deflated; things were hard enough without all this happening. After seeing Ethan in hospital I snapped. I went straight to the pub and ordered a pint of Stella. I sat in a chair by myself and watched the bubbles in that pint rising up through the sweet golden liquid into its creamy frothy head. As I was set to take that first satisfying gulp, I somehow stopped myself. What was I thinking? I ran out of the pub, leaving the pint where it was, got in my car and drove straight to an AA meeting.

Those bad experiences turned out to be a great test as, despite a close call, I held my resolve and didn't resort to the bottle. After that experience I realised that I was strong enough not to need alcohol in my life.

However, the guilt that I felt not playing for Swindon in their time of need was horrendous. The team were sinking without a trace and I knew that if I had been fully fit I maybe could have helped them out in some way. When the team were relegated I was gutted for the club, the fans, the players and most of all for Iffy. Matters weren't helped when Iffy told us that his contract would not be renewed in the summer.

There is no doubt that Iffy not only saved my career but also saved my life. If I hadn't have gone to rehab when I did then all the evidence suggests that my liver would have packed up. He was the only person to confront me over my drinking and help me out. Even when I told him during a relegation battle that I couldn't play he didn't have a go at me, he let me concentrate on getting well and as a result I will always be there for Iffy should he ever need my help.

In terms of my career the 2005–06 season was an unmitigated disaster for both Swindon Town and me. Yet that year marked a turning point in my life and I was more determined than ever to get back to being a proper professional footballer again.

14

REDISCOVERING THE GAME THAT I LOVED

With the season ending on such a low I felt a tremendous urge to finally get my act together. Even though I felt that I had wasted the last few years of my career I was still only 26 and believed that I had plenty of time left to succeed in the game.

Whilst all the lads relaxed at the end of the season I immediately started on my own pre-season to get myself fit again. I was desperate to be at good level of fitness when the team reported for duty so I devised a plan that would help me do it. I started going on 45-minute runs, and attending boxersize classes at my local leisure centre, as often as I could and the weight started to drop off me.

I also became fanatical about my diet and would only eat fresh and natural food. That meant muesli and yoghurt for breakfast, then chicken salad for lunch and something like steak and vegetables for dinner. I tried to cut out carbs and stayed away from one of my big temptations, chocolate. Such was my dedication that I even only drank tap water as I heard there were chemicals in bottled water.

It may surprise some people to know that when I was getting in shape I didn't use any supplements, such as protein shakes or creatine. I was so paranoid about any artificial substances in my body that I didn't want to touch them. I know a lot of players use supplements, and most clubs recommend them, but at that stage in my life I didn't want anything 'contaminating' my body.

I didn't want to get involved with weight training. Not only did I hate doing weights but I also didn't think that bulking up would help me as a player. Getting big is an obsession with all players these days but I don't always think that it helps. Some players in certain positions, such as centre backs or target men, do perhaps need to be broader than the rest, as those positions rely on strength. However, when positions rely on pace, putting on muscle can sometimes slow players down and it becomes counter productive.

If you look at players like Michael Owen and Craig Bellamy, and compare the size of their bodies and their speed now to when they were younger, then it tells its own story. Both were renowned as having blistering pace when they came onto the scene and they have both had their fair share of injuries over the years. Michael has hit the gym hard and noticeably put muscle on whilst Craig has stayed lean. These days Michael has lost a couple of yards of pace and it has affected what he can do on a pitch whilst Craig is still as quick as ever.

I have also heard that Arsene Wenger doesn't encourage the Arsenal players to do weights and that the boxer, Joe Calzaghe, does not use them. Arsenal players and Joe Calzaghe are of course renowned for their pace and quick hands so I definitely think there is something in it. In my case I thought that it would be sensible to concentrate on shedding fat and maintaining my speed.

During my own mini pre-season my teammate, Gareth Whalley, kindly offered to let me use his villa, near Nice in France, for a family break. I was looking forward to going but I was insistent on Pops coming along as well. Not only did I think it would be nice for him to have a break, and spend time with his grandchildren, but I also felt that I needed him there with me for support. Throughout my career his advice had always been invaluable and now I was trying to stay on the straight and narrow I thought he could help me stick to my regime.

The only problem was that Pops had never been abroad, was scared of flying, and he did not own a passport. He took a bit of persuading but when I told him that I needed him there with me, he came.

That break was fantastic and I look back on it with fond memories. Whilst I had been used to party style holidays in locations such as Jamaica, Grand Canaria and Dubai it was nice that at this stage I had a holiday in a quiet relaxed little village where there were no distractions and we could spend time together as a family.

At the crack of dawn I would go down to the local village and buy everyone baguettes and croissants for breakfast. The rest of the morning I would then spend working out by going running, on bike rides or swimming in the pool at our villa. When I was knackered we all sat down and had lunch together and spent the afternoon either messing around in the pool or watching DVDs. It was a happy time and I think Pops enjoyed his first and last holiday abroad. I'm glad that he got to spend it with his son and his grandkids, as we loved having him with us.

Slowly, but surely, I was my father's son again rediscovering the simple pleasures of life, which I had disregarded in my quest to get drunk. I was enjoying spending time with my family, watching my children grow up and realising that football was one of my great loves. It made me feel sick to think about how close I had come to losing all of these things.

Whilst everything was fantastic there was a slight issue on my return to the UK when I got caught driving at 103 miles per hour on the M4. On the day of my court case in Swindon I popped into the club quickly and was shocked to see that they were announcing the appointment of Dennis Wise as manager and Gus Poyet as his assistant. Dennis and Gus hadn't long retired from the game, and had, of course, been top players, so I couldn't quite believe I would be playing for them at Swindon Town.

As I was about to leave the ground, to make my way to court, I bumped into Dennis. Here I was, not long out of rehab and on my way to court and I was thinking 'Shit! What must he think of me?' but all he said was, 'I'll see you for pre-season'.

Those words spurred me on; Dennis Wise and Gus Poyet would be waiting for me at pre-season. It was an incentive to get myself fitter than ever. What footballer wouldn't want to impress former players of that calibre? I threw myself into training even harder, wanting to do everything and anything that I could to get fit and make a good impression.

When I reported for pre-season training, I was the fittest that I had been in years. I was back to 12 stone 8 pounds and my beer gut had been replaced by a six-pack. The first day of pre-season is usually the worst but I was looking forward to showing that I was a new man. I thought that Dennis was going to have us doing all sorts so I was shocked when he said, 'All you're going to do this morning is three exercises; 2,000 metres on the rowing machine, a 20-yard dash and a 1,000 metre run'. All the lads licked their lips, we could get all that done within 25 minutes and then be on our way home, it was music to our ears.

First up was the 2,000 metre row that we had to do as quickly as possible. As we set off Dennis stood next to us recording everything in his notebook whilst Gus urged us on. I did the 2,000 metres in 7 minutes 52 seconds, which was quite respectable. Next up was the 20-yard dash, which was my speciality, and whilst I can't recall what my time was, it was quick and I certainly showed Dennis that I could sprint.

Last and by no means least came the 1,000 metre run. Our grounds man had marked out a 500m track at the training ground so it was just two laps and that would be that. It sounded easy enough. I took off for that first lap like a bat out of hell, my technique was perfect, and I bombed around it with my legs and arms pumping away. Then as I reached 650 metres my legs started getting heavy, my heart was pounding and I was getting light headed but there was no chance of me slowing down with Gus and Dennis watching. As I came around that final bend my lungs were ready to burst but Gus was encouraging me so I put in one final push and came home in around 3 minutes 52 seconds. As I lay crashed out on the grass, with my training over for the day, Dennis recorded the time in his book. Little did I know that his book would soon become the bane of my life.

For the rest of pre-season we did those three exercises every day and we had to at least match the time recorded on the first day. The only problem was that we would soon be running six 1,000 metres back to back and every 1,000 metres you had to beat the time that you set on the first day. It was hell. I don't know how I did it but all summer I somehow managed to keep within my time for every 1,000 metres. To be honest, missing a time under Dennis Wise was not an option. If someone missed their time, and made excuses, Dennis would consult his notebook and give them a look that soon put them in their place. Another problem was that despite the fact that Dennis was around 39 years of age, and retired, he could still beat most of us in the running and he wouldn't fail to remind us of that fact if we slowed down.

Dennis was so scientific it was ridiculous. He recorded absolutely everything and opened my eyes as to how a football team could be managed. A typical day during pre-season would consist of an eight minute jog to warm up, which Dennis usually turned into a sprint leaving us knackered before we had even started. We would then concentrate on working on our core by doing resistance work on gym balls. Following that we would do our three exercises of 2,000 metre row, 20-yard dash and up to six 1,000 metre runs.

After all the lung busting cardio work we would then break for lunch. Dennis' attention to detail was legendary, he even ensured that we all ate lunch at the club and the only things available were chicken, fish, pasta and salad. It was a bit of a culture shock at first to a lot of the lads but we soon began to feel the benefits.

When lunch was over we would be back out on the training field for the rest of the afternoon doing ball work, discussing tactics, working on our shape and practising our technique. We also did a lot of work understanding everyone else's roles in the team, like the famous Ajax 'Total Football' teams used to do in the 1970s.

We usually did the technique sessions with Gus and he was ridiculous. In one drill someone would stand behind the goal and chip a ball over the crossbar to a player waiting on the edge of the penalty area. The player would have to volley the ball first time at the goal. When Gus was showing us the correct technique I swear he smashed the ball into the top corner every time, with both feet! If Gus joined in practice games he could do some crazy things with a ball, some of the goals he scored in training were out of this world.

Early on in pre-season, when we were doing a lot of running, I remember we had a guy from Holland on trial with us. For the first five days he was with us, all we did was run and he became a little fed up with it. On the sixth day he told Dennis he had a slight hamstring strain and couldn't run so Dennis said he could sit out. In the afternoon Dennis announced that we would be playing a practice game and miraculously the Dutch player recovered. He approached Dennis, boots in hand, and said he would be okay to play. Dennis kept saying to him, 'Are you sure it's okay because it's going to be a really hard afternoon?' to which the Dutch guy replied that he was now fine.

'Alright then,' Dennis replied, 'Put your trainers on, you're running!' The guy went home the next day.

In training I enjoyed our five-a-side games when we would play oldies against the youngsters. Amazingly, at only 26, I was in the oldies team but I loved it as I played with Dennis and Gus. We usually played in different positions to those we were used to which meant I tended to play at right back. Even though it was just a mess about Dennis wanted to win more than anyone and if you made a mistake he would do his nut. It was a good laugh and everyone looked forward to it.

Whilst the stuff we did on tactics and technique was top notch it wasn't anything truly revolutionary, the key to Dennis and Gus' success with us was all psychological. They built up our confidence and made us feel as if anything was possible. When you look at football it is really a simple game and a lot of it is in your head. If you are a confident player, who knows his role in the team, then you have a chance.

I also liked the fact that Dennis and Gus treated us as adults. They didn't bollock us if they could see we were trying our best and if we had an alternative point of view they were happy to speak to us about it. As a result the respect we had for them was immense, we would run through brick walls for them.

During the previous seasons I had either been playing on the wing, in the hole or up front and whilst I didn't mind where I played, my favourite position had always been as a forward. I was therefore delighted when Dennis gave me two pieces of good news. The first was that he wanted me to play up front in the forthcoming season and that if I scored over 20 goals he would pay for me to have a holiday with the family. That was exactly what I needed to hear, I would be playing in my favourite position and the manager had set me a target that I thought I had a good chance of breaking, with a nice little incentive waiting for me if I did.

The other news that Dennis had completely floored me, and if I'm honest choked me up a bit. Dennis said that he was in talks to sign Aidie Williams from Reading and that he would be the club captain but he wanted me to act as vice captain. I didn't know what to say at first; I thought he was winding me up. I had never been near the armband at any of my previous clubs and only a few months previously I had been a disgrace to professional footballers. Suddenly to have the faith of someone like Dennis Wise, who has done so much in the game, was truly mind blowing.

Whilst most people probably wouldn't have considered me for a leadership position, having known about my past, it was exactly what I needed at that time in my life. I thrived on the responsibility and it certainly made me grow up, as I wasn't just thinking about myself but also about getting the best out of the lads around me. In a way it also gave me an even greater desire to stay sober as I didn't want to let Dennis and Gus down after they had shown such great faith in me.

One week that summer that could have turned into a nightmare was when we went to play in a tournament in Ibiza. I had only been out of rehab for six months so I was terrified of all the temptations lurking everywhere in a party town like Ibiza. Thankfully I managed to stay strong and the trip was a huge success.

The first night we were in Ibiza we were told we

could have a wander around the town. Jamie Vincent, Andy Guirney, Aidie Williams and me set off and on our travels we bumped into Dennis, Gus and their assistant David Tuttle (who everyone called 'Tutts'). Dennis told Jamie and Andy Guirney to go back to the hotel, as we had a game the next day, but asked Aidie and me to stay with him.

As we walked up the strip with Dennis and Gus, I couldn't believe how many people ran out of the bars to mob the two of them. Every couple of yards they were stopping for pictures, signing autographs, engaging in some banter and it was never a hassle for them. When we walked into a bar the owner immediately sent us up to a VIP area and told a couple to move so that we could have a table.

It was another world being in the company of stars like Dennis and Gus, I couldn't believe the lengths that people would go to help them out and it certainly opened my eyes to the benefits of being a 'celebrity'. However when we sat down it was all business. This wasn't a jolly; Dennis outlined what he expected from Aidie and me as captain and vice captain and we knew we had to set an example in front of the rest of the lads.

Training in the Ibiza heat was hard work and Dennis was still fanatical about us hitting our times. Most days we would do 20 100-metre sprints in a row, which was horrendous and a few of the lads puked their guts up after it. Thankfully sprinting was my strong point so I managed to make a good impression, even if it did virtually kill me.

Even though we were in Ibiza we weren't allowed to let ourselves go, this was a serious camp. I remember one day we were all in the hotel eating dinner and I saw cream cake desserts being laid out which you could help yourself to. In a moment of weakness I went up to grab one. Just as I picked up the cream cake, Dennis and Gus walked in. Dennis took the plate out of my hand and in front of everyone said, 'You're banned from desserts!' The boys roasted me but it was little things like that which ensured I got into terrific shape.

It wasn't all work though as a few of us spent our spare time playing cards by the pool. The card school usually consisted of Dennis, Tutts, Michael Pook and me. Some of the money floating around when we were playing was ridiculous. There was Dennis, a wealthy man, at one end of the scale and Michael Pook, a youngster who was no doubt on peanuts, at the other end. This didn't matter as Dennis would shit himself more than anyone if there was big money in the pot and Pooky would happily play his hand with no fear. In one hand I won £800.00 and that sorted me right out.

Banter is always a key part to having a happy squad and there was certainly plenty of that in Ibiza. Wisey used to be covered head to toe in his naughty Prada gear, it was ridiculous and because of his height we would all wind him up saying, 'Its large boys Dennis'. He would then flash the label and give us a wink and that would set us off again.

Fair play to Dennis and Gus, they may have been in charge but they could still be one of the boys. On the last night in Ibiza we won the tournament that we had gone out to play in and everyone was obviously on a high. At the start of the week Dennis told us that on the last night we would be able to go out and let our hair down. After the game he got us together and said, 'Right lads, as promised, you can all go out on the town tonight but there is a strict curfew . . . make sure you make the flight home tomorrow. I don't care whether you go off the island or not, do what you like, but no one misses the flight tomorrow!'

That night was mental! I found out that DJ Luck and MC Neat were doing a night in one of the clubs so I bowled on down there but because I couldn't drink any alcohol, I got through 30 cans of Red Bull. I finally returned to the hotel at 7.00am and I had so much caffeine in my body that I was shaking and my heart was racing. There was no doubt that I was probably in the best state of all the lads. Some went out and got paralytic and ran off with girls and all sorts. Yet despite the carnage every single one of the boys made the flight, even if they were in a mess.

During pre-season Dennis signed my old Bristol City strike partner, Lee Peacock, from Sheffield Wednesday. It's fair to say that Lee and I didn't really see eye-to-eye when we were together at Bristol and at times we barely spoke to each other. When we played together we didn't really have a partnership, we were just two individuals, even though the year we were together Lee scored 15 goals and I scored 17. On paper we should have worked well as he was a big strong target man, with an eye for goal, and I was a nippy, skilful player. I won't lie, I wasn't really looking forward to being reunited with Lee but when he arrived it was obvious that we had both matured a lot since our days at Bristol. We became close on and off the pitch and struck up a great partnership that really flourished in the early part of the season.

With the season set to get underway I was like a dog let off its leash. I couldn't wait to get going to show the fans the new and improved Christian Roberts. Aidie Williams had picked up an injury towards the end of pre-season meaning that for the first six games I would captain the side.

It could be said that those six games were the highlight of my playing career. Not only did I play out of my skin, but I also captained the team to six successive wins. We started with a 1–0 away win over Hartlepool, then beat Barnet, Rochdale, Darlington, Stockport and Chester. Wisey told the press after the Barnet game: 'The one person I think you have to pick out tonight was Christian Roberts. Unfortunately he didn't score but his overall performance was magnificent. I've just said it to him in the dressing room in front of everyone and I know the others call him my son, but that's not a problem. I was so pleased for him and he deserved a goal.'

I scored my first goal, since I had left rehab, against Darlington and the rush I felt when that ball hit the back of the net was electric. This was what it was all about, captaining a successful team at the top of the league, under an inspirational manager and scoring goals. I was back in love with football and it had replaced the buzz that alcohol used to give me. My partnership with Lee Peacock was really coming together by now and the local press said: 'In Christian Roberts and Lee Peacock, they have one of the best forward pairings in the division, and both of them showed plenty of movement and ability to hold the ball up.'

Following our win against Stockport, where I scored again, I was really pleased that my leadership qualities were being recognised. The *Western Daily Press* called me a 'Welsh warrior' and that made me feel on top of the world. Whilst Aidie Williams eventually got back to fitness, and took over the captaincy, I was proud of my stint in the role and I'm sure I surprised a few people as well.

Everything under Dennis and Gus went up a couple of notches compared to what we had been used to. Travelling to away games became more comfortable, the hotels were a lot nicer, the food that the club supplied was fresh and healthy and it goes without saying that the training sessions were immense. We all looked forward to going into work every day, as Dennis and Gus would literally fill us to the brim with confidence through their enthusiasm and energy. If we needed bringing back down to earth then Dennis would do it but I remember feeling good about myself at this time. I was happy on and off the pitch and it had been a long time since I could have said that.

Another great addition to our team was when Dennis signed his old England teammate, Paul Ince. We couldn't believe it when we heard that Incey was joining us. Yes, he was getting on a bit, but this guy was a legend who had played for Manchester United and Inter Milan. Swindon Town don't sign players of the calibre of Paul Ince every day so everyone associated with the club couldn't wait to see him in action.

Incey made his debut for us away to Wrexham and the night before the game, whilst we were having dinner, he told us tales from his time at Man United and Inter Milan. All the players were like star struck kids listening to his stories and it was a pleasure to have him with us.

Even though he was a legend in the game, that didn't stop us from giving him some banter. When the conversation turned to wives and girlfriends I piped up, 'You've been with your wife a long time and have been all over the world, whilst she has stayed at home, you must trust her?' Incey's face went from messing around to one of absolute seriousness. 'You know what I mean Incey?' I said, trying to dig myself out of a hole, 'Your wife could be doing anything whilst you are away and you would never know'. To our amazement a worried looking Paul Ince jumped off the table and called his wife. That had us in absolute stitches!

Everything was going well but my knee started bothering me and it meant that I was unable to train some days. Gus paid for me, out of his own pocket, to see a specialist that he had used in Spain when he had played for Real Zaragoza. The specialist was top notch and had even treated the former Barcelona player, Samuel Eto. Not only did Gus sort me out with flights, the appointment with the consultant and a place to stay but he also hired a driver to take me wherever I wanted. I had only known Gus for a few weeks but he didn't think twice about paying for me to have my injury sorted out. The consultant put some gel injections in my knee, which meant that I missed a few games, but it rectified the problem and I was grateful.

Dennis and Gus were genuine people and it was a pleasure to play for them. For some reason they both took to me and helped me however they could. I don't know why they were so good to me, maybe they saw me as a project or maybe Dennis could relate to me as he has, of course, had his own ups and downs during his playing career, but for whatever reason I am so grateful to the two of them. Playing under them was the happiest that I had ever been playing football.

Unfortunately all good things end and Dennis and Gus left Swindon to join Leeds United in November. When I heard that they were leaving I was gutted. Dennis rang me personally and explained that sometimes in life you get opportunities that you can't turn down. He also said that Ken Bates, who was a friend of Dennis', and was now Chairman of Leeds following his spell at Chelsea, had personally asked Dennis to do him a favour. I was so upset when Dennis confirmed he was going. For once everything was coming together on and off the pitch but after only four short months working with Dennis and Gus they were gone.

It says a lot about my relationship with the two of them that they have kept in touch. I used to speak to Dennis regularly but haven't spoken to him for a little bit but I know that when I speak to him again he will be the same, happy-go-lucky little cockney giving out some dodgy banter. On the other hand I speak to Gus quite a lot and when I told him I was writing a book, and asked him for a few words, he said the following about our time at Swindon together:

> Dennis knew all about Christian's problems before we went to Swindon. He said he was going to give him a chance but we weren't quite sure what to expect but he did great as soon as we arrived. He did everything that we asked of him, and more, and everyday he kept improving to such an extent that Dennis and me were getting very excited, as we knew we had a player on our hands.
>
> Christian had arrived at pre-season slightly heavy but after three weeks he had his top off all the time

showing off his six-pack. Dennis knew how hard he was working and wanted to give him something back as a reward, so he made him vice-captain, and he didn't let us down. He did really well as captain and we were very happy with him. There is no doubt he could have played at a higher level and when I left Swindon I followed his career closely. Dennis and me had a great time at Swindon, we had put together a really good group of fit, talented players and Christian was a big part of that, it was hard to leave as we knew they were going to be successful.

With Dennis and Gus gone, the rumour mill suggested that former Southampton manager, Paul Sturrock, was going to take over. I had a few friends who had played under him before and to be honest I wasn't too keen on what I had heard. Sturrock was renowned as being an old school manager, who was stuck in his ways, whilst Dennis had been a breath of fresh air. He had introduced us to things that we had never seen or done before and as a result it had been exciting working for him.

After Dennis had left I did initially find it hard to adjust to Sturrock as it was difficult to go from a forward thinking manager to a guy who seemed to be rooted in the dark ages. Dennis's regime had opened my eyes to how a football club could be run and I have to admit I didn't really have any desire to go backwards.

When Sturrock came in I was still speaking to Dennis regularly and was eager to learn everything that I could from him. Dennis was adamant that I should be playing at a higher level and at one point there was even some talk of me joining him at Leeds, but for whatever reason it didn't materialise.

Everything was a bit harder under Sturrock than it had been under Dennis and Gus. All of a sudden our travelling became a bit of a pain, most of the time we wouldn't reach our hotel for away trips until 11.00pm on the Friday night before a game so we would be knackered. When we got there we would find that the hotels weren't as comfortable as they had been under Dennis either. It's not as if we were demanding luxury but we did at least expect to stay in a place that was clean. The food we ate also wasn't of the same standard as it had been previously. Sturrock would insist on us eating a Scottish dish called 'Stovie' (mincemeat and mashed potato). It was all right but not on a par with the food we had become accustomed to. It may be that the club decided Dennis' regime had cost too much to sustain so they made cut backs but it was difficult for the players to accept.

One thing that did annoy me when Sturrock came in was that he stripped me of the vice-captaincy. I was injured for his first game in charge so he made Jamie Vincent vice-captain and then stuck with him. It was never a subject that Sturrock discussed with me but I was bitterly disappointed, as I loved having that position of responsibility. Losing the vice-captaincy was a bitter blow but the most important thing was winning promotion and I was determined not to rock the boat.

Sturrock's approach was certainly different to Dennis' but to be fair he was a good manager, as he got results, and that is what it is all about at the end of the day. Whilst I didn't have the same bond with him that I enjoyed with the previous management I respected him, and to a degree, I enjoyed my time playing under him.

A downside of playing under Sturrock however was that he decided that he wanted to utilise my pace on the wing so I was removed from my favoured striker's berth. Firstly I was put out on the right wing but when he signed Jon-Paul McGovern I was shifted to the left. My strike partner, Lee Peacock, was moved into centre midfield which seemed a bit strange as a few weeks previously we had been heralded as one of the best forward partnerships in the league. As a result of my change of position, my goals dried up and any hope I had of reaching 20 goals soon disappeared. I did however finish the season with 13 goals, which I was relatively pleased with.

One of the games where I played on the wing was shown on Sky and as we were driving back to Swindon, on the team coach, my phone rang. It was Gus. When I answered he shouted, 'What the fuck are you doing playing on the wing and why is Lee Peacock playing centre mid?' We had a laugh about it, and it was nice to see that Gus was still following Swindon Town and me.

In the last few games of the season we looked certain to win promotion after we defeated Mansfield Town, 2–0. That result meant that all we needed to do was to get one point from our last two games and we would go up. It didn't go to plan as we crashed to a 1–0 defeat to Bristol Rovers, thanks to a 30 yard wonder strike, and that meant that we needed to get a draw against Walsall in our final game of the season. Walsall would be a tough proposition as they were also going for promotion.

As it turned out if we drew with Walsall we would get promoted and they would be champions. On the day we went one nil up, when Jerrel Ifil scored with a great header in the first half. Walsall went on to equalise in the second half and what followed was one of the most bizarre games of football I have ever played in. With both teams needing just a point we were both reluctant to go for a winner so the game turned into a bit of a farce. Both teams passed the ball sideways and backwards and it wouldn't surprise me to learn that there wasn't a single shot in the last 20 minutes. Whilst there was no conspiracy between the teams to settle for a draw we both knew that all we needed was for everyone on both teams to be sensible and we would all benefit.

When the final whistle went the County Ground went nuts. The Swindon and Walsall fans were singing their hearts out and the two teams were hugging each other and dancing together. It was a lovely atmosphere and it was nice that the two of us went up together. At one point I think I was hugging a Walsall player and we had our arms around each other's shoulders bouncing up and down in front of the crowd.

After celebrating out on the pitch we all went back to the changing room to continue the celebrations. As the champagne started flying everywhere I hid in the corner with towels over my body so that the alcohol wouldn't touch me. It was a reminder that whilst everything in my personal and professional life was back on track, I still could not let alcohol anywhere near me.

Earlier that season I had gone out on the town with the players and when it was my round, I bought the boys some Buds. I was of course sticking to sparkling water. When the barman put one of the bottles down on the bar it started frothing over and my immediate reaction was to put my lips around the top of the bottle to stop it. Just as I knelt down to do it I suddenly realised what I was doing and leapt back. It was a natural reaction and I hadn't even thought that it was a bottle of beer but if I had that one sip I'm sure I would have followed that up with about 20 beers. It was a sign that I wasn't quite ready to be around alcohol yet.

As a result, whilst all the boys hit the town to celebrate, I drove back to Cardiff and spent the night with my family. I sensed that I was gradually getting a grip over my addiction and knew how to control it at last. Finally my career and my life were back on track.

15

THINGS TAKE A TURN FOR THE WORSE

Now that we were back in League One, and had a good squad and manager, I was confident that we could be dark horses for promotion. I was also looking forward to playing in that division sober for the first time in my career to show what I could do. Things didn't quite turn out as I had planned.

When we reported back it was a vastly different pre-season regime to Wisey's. As I mentioned previously, Dennis had been scientific and recorded everything, whilst Sturrock's pre-season consisted of long runs.

We went out to Austria to play a few games and whilst we were there I realised that I had a problem with my knee. After every training session I would be in agony and I was struggling to train every day. In the back of my mind I realised that it was something serious but I made the excuse that it was due to the hard ground, and the intensity of the training sessions, and that once we were back home it would sort itself out.

Yet when we returned to Swindon the pain refused to subside. I tried everything to treat it from physio to injections but nothing would take the edge off. I went through painkillers like Smarties and I must have been taking at least 10 a day. With the pain refusing to go away I soon realised that there was no way that I could continue to train every day.

My knee problems all stemmed from the injury that I sustained when I was 11 years old. Back then the surgeon had taken two thirds of the cartilage out of my knee; this would have been fine as long as I didn't suffer any further injuries to it, which unfortunately I did. I had two more knee operations at Cardiff, one at Bristol and one at Swindon and consequently I was left with no cartilage in my knee whatsoever. Without it providing any cushioning the bones were grinding against each other every time I ran. When you are training and playing almost every single day this can cause serious damage to your knee as it wears down the bones and can leave you unable to walk at times.

I knew that by training every day I was not only doing myself more damage but it was also making it more difficult for me to be fit for games. With this in mind I set up a meeting with Dick the physio and Paul Sturrock to air my concerns. To be fair to Sturrock he was very sympathetic and as long as I would be fit to play he didn't seem to mind that I couldn't train all the time. We therefore agreed that on Mondays I would go in but would cycle or work in the pool. On Tuesdays I would train properly but would then have Wednesdays and Thursdays off before training at a medium level on Fridays. Thankfully this routine worked for a while and allowed me to play two games a week.

I was, of course, worried that I may not be as fit as I needed to be, due to not training every day, but consoled myself by thinking about players such as

Ledley King and Paul McGrath who suffered from similar problems and still went on to have great careers.

Whilst I played through the pain barrier, our form over the first half of the season was up and down. We drew too many games and failed to put a run of wins together. Two games that do come to mind in that spell however are the games at Swansea and Leeds.

As an ex-Cardiff player I was never going to be popular in West Wales and I didn't really endear myself to the Swansea fans when, before the game, I gave an interview and said: 'I have no relationship with the Swansea fans and I don't expect anything but abuse. I am a Cardiff boy and proud of it and I don't even like going down there.'

Kaid Mohammed, who was one of my good friends at Swindon, was also from Cardiff so we were both looking forward to playing against Swansea at the Liberty Stadium. As Cardiff boys it's fair to say that we were keen to give Swansea a good seeing to.

On the coach, on the way to the game, Kaid and me were talking about how amazing it would be if we could get a goal during the game. Kaid asked me, 'Would you do the Ayatollah if you score?'

I cockily replied, 'Of course I would!' Despite my bravado I don't think Kaid believed that I would actually do it.

The Ayatollah is a gesture that Cardiff City fans do, which consists of patting the palms of your hands up and down on your head. To do the Ayatollah at the Liberty Stadium, as a former Cardiff City player, would be the ultimate wind up and after the abuse I had received from Swansea fans over the years I was determined to do it.

Predictably, during the game, the Swans fans booed my every touch and screamed all sorts of filth at me. I felt like a pantomime villain but if anything the abuse spurred me on to ram it back down their throats.

Unfortunately Swansea went 1–0 up and hearing all those Swans fans celebrating made me sick. Not long afterwards I picked up the ball just outside the box, I burnt off the defender who was marking me before arrowing a screamer into the top corner, job done! I ran to celebrate with the Swindon fans but the Swansea fans' boos were drowning out the sound of the loyal 100 who had travelled down to support us. I looked over at the bench and saw Kaid laughing doing the Ayatollah. As I ran back to the halfway line I did it back to him and the place blew up. I swear, all hell broke loose, the fans went bananas, and it got so bad I actually feared for my safety.

One thing that I hadn't really thought through when I did the Ayatollah was the fact that I was playing on the wing. That meant that not only was I right next to the crowd, so I could hear every curse and every threat, but every time I took a throw in I got pelted.

About five minutes after my goal Swansea scored what would turn out to be the winner. At the end of the game Paul Sturrock went ballistic at me as he felt that I had riled the crowd and that had wound up the Swansea players. I thought that was rubbish but I kept my thoughts to myself.

After the final whistle I was keen to get away from the ground sharpish but typically I was randomly selected for a drugs test. It was the first and only test of my career and it had to come at a time like this. As I drank bottle after bottle of water, so that I could pee, Pops and Janine were waiting upstairs in the bar for me. Pops had the thickest Cardiff accent around so he was careful not to open his mouth as a Swansea fan may have given him some grief. As Pops and Janine stood at the bar they heard a load of Swansea fans discussing how they were going to sort me out once I left the ground.

Janine rang to tell me what was going on and by this stage I had gathered that a little mob had already gathered outside the player's entrance. I told Janine to drive our car right in front of the ground, get in the passenger seat and I would then run out, jump in the car and speed away. As I was preparing to make a run for it I told a policeman, who was going to shepherd me to my car, that there was no way I was going to stop at any red lights until I was out of Swansea. He was sympathetic and told me I had to do what I needed to do to get out of there all in one piece.

As I sprinted out of the entrance of the ground it took a few seconds for the waiting mob to realise that it was me. By the time it dawned on them that I was the man they were waiting to stone I was in my car and wheel spinning away so I could just make out this bunch of tossers screaming at me in my rear view mirror. I wasn't taking any chances though and didn't stop at a red light until I got back to the safety of Cardiff.

Doing the Ayatollah caused me a bit of bother, and made my manager furious with me, but would I do it again if I had the chance? Of course I would, which Cardiff City fan wouldn't?

Shortly after the Swansea game we travelled to Elland Road to play Leeds United who were flying high near the top of the table. Leeds were of course managed by our former manager, Dennis Wise and his assistant Gus Poyet. Unfortunately we lost the game 2–1 but afterwards I popped into the manager's office to speak to Dennis and Gus. It was great to see them again and I thanked them for all that they had done for me. It was hard, as being with the two of them made me realise what I was missing out on.

With the team hovering around mid-table in January 2008 we were faced with yet another managerial change. Paul Sturrock's former club, Plymouth Argyle, wanted him to return to the club and he unsurprisingly jumped at the chance.

After having played under Dennis Wise and Paul Sturrock it was disappointing when the club decided to appoint Maurice Malpas as manager. I absolutely hated the man, not only did I think he was a poor manager but I also felt that he was unbelievably arrogant and ill equipped for the job.

I remember when I first heard that Malpas was taking over, Hasney Aljofree, one of my teammates, called me and said, 'You'll never guess who the club have appointed as manager?'

His tone wasn't one which led me to believe it was anyone exciting so my heart sank, 'Who?' I replied in a weary tone already fearing the worst.

In the most downbeat manner that you can imagine Hasnee said, 'Maurice Malpas!'

'Who the hell is that?' Hasney explained that Maurice was regarded as a bit of a legend up in Scotland and that when he had been a youngster at Dundee United he had actually taken Malpas' place in the team and as a result forced him into retirement. 'Good luck with him then,' I sympathetically said.

Malpas had done nothing in English football and this was going to be his first managerial job. I was staggered that he had been appointed but I was prepared to give him a chance. Unfortunately it was immediately apparent that the guy didn't have a clue.

If we had moaned about the travelling, food and hotels under Sturrock then, when Malpas joined, it sank to new depths. The travel was haphazard and uncomfortable, the food was unhealthy slop and the hotels were shocking. Again, we weren't asking for the best but this sort of poor preparation doesn't put footballers in the best frame of mind and consequently standards started to drop. Only a year before the training ground had been buzzing and everyone had been eager to get to work, but now the place was miserable. It felt as if the soul had been ripped out of the club. The club had no banter, energy, spark or indeed anything that resembled a pulse.

It was also obvious that Malpas didn't rate me. In his first four games in charge he didn't select me once in his starting line up. When he finally picked me, for a game against Luton, I showed him just how wrong he was with a goal that the press called 'a stunning individual effort'. I got the ball out on the wing, skinned the old Spurs defender Chris Perry and then rifled a screamer into the corner of the goal. After that he couldn't really leave me out but he started to make life difficult for me.

When Malpas first came into the club he wanted to know why I wasn't training every day. Dick and I told him about my situation and the routine I had been doing under Paul Sturrock but he wasn't interested, he wanted me to train every single day. This meant that come game day my knee would be shot, some days I would be limping to the ground and would need intensive treatment to be able to run at three quarter pace.

In spite of the fact that I thought Malpas was rubbish, I showed him respect and tried to get on with my job of being a player. The only problem was I couldn't always do that. To be able to train I was having injections, tablets, physio, stretches and I even tried sleeping at a certain angle, but nothing could ease the pain. It was so bad that after a game I struggled to walk for days afterwards. It wasn't a sharp pain but a constant dull ache that kept me awake at night.

In the end it was obvious, even to Malpas, that I could only train twice a week, if that. Despite this, when he knew that I could barely walk, he demanded that I turn up at the club, even if I couldn't train. I would sit in the gym for 20 minutes, in agony, unable to do much thinking, 'What is the point of me being here?' I could understand it if I was having all sorts of treatment and help for my knee but I wasn't, he simply did it to make a point.

Dick, the physio, did everything that he could for me but sometimes I'm sure even he didn't believe me when I told him that I couldn't train. Unfortunately, in the days when I was drinking, I had used up a lot of Dick's trust by skiving off training due to hangovers so he didn't always know if I was lying or telling the truth. At times this didn't particularly help my cause in getting his backing to persuade Malpas that I couldn't train. I had brought that on myself as I was like the boy who cried wolf and when I was actually telling the truth, and in dire need to miss training, I had already used up all my excuses.

During my time at Swindon I had spent so much time with Dick, through my alcoholism and my knee trouble, that he was almost like a father figure to me. He had seen my ups and downs and he probably knew me better than anyone. We sometimes had our differences but Dick knew I could be a raw cat and knew how to take me. He was a lovely fella as well and would do almost anything for me but it was frustrating when he didn't appreciate the level of pain that I was in.

By March I knew that I was in serious trouble with my knee as nothing was working, and I began to worry that my time in the game could be at an end. On 26 February 2008, after a 2–2 draw at Oldham, I remember that as I limped off the pitch I knew I had made my knee much worse. The pain had reached a new level of intensity and for the next few days I couldn't walk.

On St David's Day we faced Leeds United at the County Ground. Dennis and Gus had departed Leeds by this stage, with Gus going to Spurs and Dennis to Newcastle. Despite being unable to walk the day before the game, for some reason I woke up on the Saturday and my knee felt all right so I was able to play. We lost the game 1–0 but I thought that I had played reasonably well. It wasn't the best game that I had ever played but it was far from my worst.

However, after the match I was crippled by pain in my knee. I decided that with a game coming up against Huddersfield on Tuesday night, that rather than go home, I would spend the next few days in Swindon getting treatment to give myself a chance of playing. That night my knee ballooned up and I again couldn't walk the next day. On the Sunday I had some intensive physio, injections and got through a cocktail of pills and whilst by the Monday I could walk, I still couldn't run. I continued to have treatment throughout the day and thankfully on the Tuesday morning I could run and was fit to face Huddersfield. I had been through two days of hell to get to that stage but was now ready to play.

Yet when Malpas read the team out before the game I was on the bench and I was fuming. My performance against Leeds had been decent and I certainly didn't feel that it warranted him dropping me.

I marched down to his office, ready to tear his head off, and said, whilst trying to contain myself, 'What's going on Gaffer?' He could tell I was pissed off and explained that he was resting me because he knew my knee had been playing me up. I was disappointed but I accepted his explanation and when we were in the dug out before the game I apologised to him for my rant.

We ended up winning the game 3–2 but I only got on the pitch for the last couple of minutes, which I was a bit annoyed about as I had worked so hard to get myself fit. It says it all about Malpas' man management that when I came on he took off Ashikodi, who had himself only come on after 78 minutes. I consoled myself that having hardly played, and with a few days of rest ahead of me, that I should at least be fully fit for Saturday's game.

In the changing room after the match Aidie Williams, who was now the reserve team manager, came in and read out who would be travelling with the reserves to play Exeter the following day. I wasn't really listening, as due to my knee I rarely played for the reserves, but I was stunned when I heard my name mentioned. I had only played a few minutes that night as I was being rested and suddenly I found out I would be playing for the reserves the following day, a day when I was meant to be resting my crippled knee.

I stormed out of the dressing room, for the second time that day, and barged into the manager's office.

'Can I have a word?' I shouted as I marched in.

'No,' said Malpas with a smarmy look.

'Well I want a fucking word!' I snapped back at him. His attitude towards me only served to make me angrier. 'What's going on here?' I said, 'You told me I was being rested tonight and now I'm in the reserves tomorrow.'

He looked me up and down with a smirk on his face and said, 'Well if you don't like it don't play'.

'What?' I shouted, barely able to contain my anger.

'You heard me, if you don't like it, don't play. If you don't play I'll just fine you.'

I couldn't believe what I was hearing. He knew about my knee troubles, and that was supposedly the reason I had been dropped that night, yet now he wanted me to play in the reserves the next day. I couldn't work it out, it seemed he was showing me a total lack of respect and wasn't being straight with me. It also seemed that he wasn't taking my knee problems seriously. As I said, he was always dragging me up to the training ground when he knew that I was suffering and half the time I swear he did it out of spite.

After a shouting match with Malpas I went to find Dick and told him that he needed to book me in to see a consultant to have a look at my knee. I told him that I would be calling him straight after the reserve game the next day and I wanted him to have a date for when I could see the consultant.

The next day I played 60 minutes against my old club Exeter before the pain in my knee forced me to hobble off. Straight after the game, whilst Aidie was still giving the team talk, I was on the phone to Dick to make sure he had booked my appointment.

On 12 March 2008 I went to Harley Street, in London, with Dick to see the consultant, Jonathan Webb. The news wasn't good, Jonathan informed me that my knee was in a terrible state and he couldn't believe that I had been playing on it. He said that I needed a serious operation that would leave me with only a 5% chance of ever playing again. When I saw the scans of my knee it looked black, almost as if it was rotting away.

As I sat in that room trying to process the bad news Dick turned to me and said, 'Chris, I'm sorry. I underestimated you'. I was welling up inside and felt like hugging and punching him at the same time. I appreciated his apology but at times that season I felt that he hadn't been pushing my case hard enough to persuade Malpas that I needed more rest.

My operation was done two weeks after my appointment and I knew that the odds were stacked heavily against me ever kicking a ball again. The surgeon drilled a hole into the bone in my knee to create a bleed, which he hoped would provide a replacement cartilage so that there would at least be some form of cushioning between my knee joints. The op was a long shot but it had worked previously on other footballers so I was keeping my fingers crossed that it would be a success.

When I woke up from my op I was greeted by a female nurse who spoke with a man's voice. That spun me out a bit and for a few hours I thought that the drugs I was on were messing with my mind but in the end it turned out that the nurse was a transsexual. I have nothing at all against gay people, and that nurse was lovely to me, nothing was too much trouble, but I didn't half think I was losing the plot.

Returning home, following my surgery, was difficult as I was on crutches and was told that I must not, under any circumstances, put any weight on my knee for the next two months. Janine had already arranged to take the kids to Disneyland so I came back to an empty house and I think I miscalculated how much I needed someone home with me. Making food and drink for myself was a nightmare as I would be hopping around trying not to spill anything but the worst part was being left by myself with my thoughts. I was desperately lonely and as all my friends and family were in work during the day, I would be left lying on the settee letting things fester in my mind.

Thankfully, as always, my old man came through for me and I used to look forward to spending Saturdays with him. He would take me up the bookies so we could place a few bets and then we would go back home and watch sport all day. We wouldn't put big money on, and we rarely won anything, but it was nice to spend some time together.

The rest of the season was a write off for me but I was hopeful that I would know whether I could play again by the start of pre-season.

16

A YEAR TO FORGET

Following the operation my progress was painfully slow, I didn't seem to have any reduction in pain whatsoever. The surgeon reassured me that I would still feel discomfort for a while, as I had undergone a serious surgical procedure, and it would take time to settle, but in the back of my mind I was starting to come to terms with the fact that my career was over.

Before pre-season I was so fed up that Janine suggested that we have a break in Dubai. It was nice to escape and I was having such a good time, away from the pressure-cooker environment of constantly thinking about my knee and career, that at one point I thought about packing it in and staying over there. However, I finally came to my senses and vowed to try every treatment available to try to play again. Whilst I knew that it was a long shot, I returned to the UK with a new found hunger to get back to playing football any way that I possibly could.

The day after we returned from Dubai I had to report to Swindon for pre-season. I was, of course, a long way from joining in with the lads but I went up to see Dick to get his view on the state of my knee. My mood drastically changed when I saw that Malpas was still around and that not only was he treating me with complete disdain, but I had also not been assigned a squad number. This meant that even if I did get fit it was obvious I was not in his plans anyway. It was hardly the incentive a footballer, who is battling to save his career, needs to put himself through the pain barrier.

I went to Swindon most days for physio, cycling and water work but the knee was not improving. It was desperately frustrating because there seemed to be no end in sight. It wasn't just the physical pain that was killing me; mentally it was tough as I didn't know how much longer I would have to put myself through it all. Every day seemed to be a relentless slog of intense agony.

By the end of August I went to see the surgeon in his Bristol office. We discussed the state of my knee, and my rehab, and I told the surgeon that I couldn't handle that level of pain and wanted to know if there was anything else he could do. He said that there was nothing more he could do and that the pain wasn't going to improve, if anything it would get worse, and if I continued to play I ran a high risk of crippling myself. With that advice ringing in my ears we agreed that it would probably be sensible to call time on my playing career.

I walked into his office as a professional footballer but I walked out on the scrap heap at only 28 years of age. It was a strange feeling as although I was obviously upset, it was also a relief at the same time, as I knew I wouldn't have to put up with the pain and the uncertainty anymore. My head was spinning as after finally getting sober, and feeling fit for the first time in years, I could never grace a professional football pitch again.

For the next couple of weeks, even though I was still contracted to Swindon Town, I didn't need to go in as the club had accepted the surgeon's advice and were in the process of negotiating my pay off with their insurers before my contract could be officially terminated on 1 October 2008.

In a home game against Millwall I said my goodbyes to the Swindon fans when I walked around the pitch at half time. It really hit me during that walk, as the fans chanted my name, that this was it. My time in the game was over and I have to admit I shed a few tears.

Football was all that I had ever known, so suddenly having to think of an alternative career was frightening. Thankfully, even before my contract was officially terminated, I was approached by a sports management company and asked to look after the football side of the business. This initially appealed to me, so for a few weeks I helped them out with scouting and attending meetings with clients.

One night in early September I went to watch my two friends, Jason Bowen and Steve Jenkins, play for Newport County. Ten minutes from the end of the game my brother Matthew called to tell me that Pops had gone into hospital as he had been suffering from pains in his leg. I knew that my old man must have been in agony to go into hospital as he was as hard as an old boot and would not have sought treatment unless absolutely necessary.

I rushed up the hospital to see what the problem was but when I got there Pops was told that he could go home but needed to go back in for tests the next day. He seemed to be all right and if anything he seemed quite upbeat.

The next morning I took him back up to the hospital to have some tests and afterwards took him home where I placed him in his favourite spot, on the settee in his living room, in front of the fire. I made him some soup and he seemed quite happy relaxing there.

Having seen him appear to be pain free, I started to relax and hoped that everything would be fine. However, the next day, at 4am, he was rushed back to the hospital. He was in so much distress that the doctor decided to keep him under observation until he received his test results so that they could monitor him and regularly give him painkillers.

Over the next two weeks the whole Roberts family took it in turns to visit Pops. On occasions like this it was a blessing that there were so many of us as we could all constantly check on him and make sure he was comfortable. As I didn't have to work 9–5 like the others, I spent a lot of time with him during those hours. I would also pop up last thing at night to make sure he was off to sleep without any problems.

For a time he seemed to be feeling a little better, no doubt due to the pain killing medication that he was on and we would chat as we had always done. Two weeks after he had been admitted I received a phone call to get up the hospital as they had finally received Pops' test results. I had just left the hospital but I did the quickest u–turn ever and raced back to be by his side within minutes of leaving him.

I vividly recall that as I entered the room Pops was lying in his bed and my uncle was standing next to him looking visibly upset. As I burst in I was anxious to know what was wrong, so blurted out, 'What's the matter Pops? What's wrong?'

As always he was unflustered and not one to over react so he tried to calm me down, 'Woah woah woah, calm down, it's nothing!'

My uncle looked at me, and then at Pops, and said, 'Come on Rich, it's not nothing, you need to tell him'.

At that instant my heart sank and I knew I was about to receive bad news. I started to look out of the window as I couldn't bear to look at my old man as he spoke as I knew I would probably break down and I didn't want to cry in front of him. After a pause that seemed to take an eternity he finally spoke, 'I've had it! I've got cancer of the liver and lungs. They can't treat it. I'm going to die'.

At first I couldn't take it in. This couldn't be happening. I didn't say anything and kept staring out of the window, biting my lip with my eyes watering. I knew that if I stayed in that room for a moment longer I would crack so I walked off to find his nurse in the hope that she would tell me that there was something that could be done. When I finally found her she confirmed my worst fears. My Dad was going to die, there was nothing that could be done and they didn't know how long he had left.

I remember I sat down with my head in my hands and tears streaming down my cheeks. Inside I was screaming, 'FUCK! NO, NO, NO! PLEASE DON'T TAKE POPS FROM ME!' I refused to believe that nothing could be done, this was my Dad, he had always been indestructible in my eyes and I could not accept that within a matter of weeks he might no longer be with us.

As I was the first out of my brothers and sisters to

hear the news I was left with the arduous task of breaking the bad news to each of them. That was heartbreaking in itself as I had to endure six separate phone calls where I knew I was delivering the worst news that each of my siblings had ever heard. We were all devastated.

The next day I went in to see Pops and I was determined to have a proper chat with him. I wanted to thank him for everything that he had ever done for me and let him know how much I loved him. I now recognised and appreciated how hard he must have worked to have fed and clothed us all as kids. I remembered how he had been to watch every single one of my games as a kid and would travel with me up and down the country, even though we probably couldn't afford the petrol, just so I had a chance of a better life. Even when I became a professional he had always been a shoulder to cry on or someone I could rely on if I was in trouble. One time I lost £1,500.00 playing cards, and I was in deep trouble, but he told me not to worry and gave me the cash to pay off the debt. Another time, when I was in deep financial shit, the gearbox on my car went and I found out that it would cost £4,500.00 to fix, a sum that I could not afford at the time but again he helped to dig me out of a hole. I was supposed to be a professional footballer on good money, and he was the workingman, but he never complained. He was an amazing human being.

I have lost count of the number of times over the years I had got myself into trouble and I would say to him 'Pops, you're going to kill me but . . .'

He wouldn't even bat an eyelid as he gave me his cash card and would say, 'I don't care, take what you need'. He was so proud of being a Dad and helping his family out that whenever I thanked him he would say, 'What are Dads for?'

I had been a terrible kid at times but Pops never lost faith in me. When everyone else berated me, he would tell me to keep my head up, but if I needed a talking to he would tell me bluntly that I had messed up.

Unfortunately when I went to see him to thank him for everything that he had done for me he was half asleep so I whispered, 'Can we have a proper chat tomorrow?' to which he nodded his head. As I left the hospital I was happy that we would be able to talk about everything and he would know not only how much he meant to me, but also what a great example of being a father he had set me. With my own kids I knew I had messed up over the years, due to my alcoholism, but now I was sober I did try to emulate my father.

Tragically I never got to have that conversation with my father. Overnight his condition deteriorated rapidly and by the morning he was virtually in a coma. When he did come around he was confused, incoherent and didn't know who I was. Over the course of the next week his condition kept going downhill and it ripped me apart to see this proud man have to suffer so much. It sounds bad to say it but I was waiting for him to die, I didn't want him to be in pain anymore. I still visited three times a day but I cut my visits to 10 minutes each time, as seeing him wasting away made me terribly upset.

What killed me was that after every visit I didn't know if it would be the last time that I would ever see him. On those visits there would be no conversation between us as Pops would be asleep so I would simply stare at him helplessly knowing that no matter what any of us did he was going to die. When I attended AA meetings I used to confide in everyone there how worried I was that when my Dad died I would return to the bottle. I did not know how I could handle his loss.

When my contract at Swindon was finally terminated on 1 October 2008, it barely registered. I was consumed with anger and grief over my Dad's situation, nothing else mattered to me. Eventually Pops was moved to a high dependency unit so nurses could keep a constant eye on him, but he continued to slip away from us before our eyes.

On 8 October 2008 Matthew and me went to see him at around 1.10pm. As we left shortly afterwards, I remember telling my brother, 'He seems alright, he doesn't appear to be in too much pain'. I had to attend a meeting with the sports management company I was helping out, and Matthew needed to go back to work, but as we set off we received a phone call at around 1.35pm saying that we needed to get back up the hospital quickly. I drove like a maniac through the streets of Cardiff, and a journey that should normally have taken at least 10 minutes took four minutes flat. When we got to the hospital I skidded into the car park, left my car without paying, and sprinted as fast as my knee would allow me up to his ward. By 1.45pm I was by his bedside.

When I arrived Pops wasn't awake and he was struggling to breathe. There seemed to be a long pause between each breath and when he did inhale air he made a choking sound. The nurse told me that he didn't have long but he seemed to keep hanging on as if he was waiting for the rest of the family to arrive so he could say goodbye. I think that he knew we would all get there so he kept fighting, which was typical of him.

By 1.55pm Daryl, David, Nathan, Michael, Sacha and my Mum had joined Matthew and me at the hospital. We were all hugging and crying and Sacha, in particular, found it hard to come to terms with.

A few minutes before 2.00pm the whole family went to my father's bedside to pay our last respects. I stood on the left hand side of the bed, alongside Matthew and Sacha, whilst Michael, Nathan and my Mum were at the foot of the bed and Daryl and David were stood to the right hand side. I remember looking at the clock on the wall and the time was 1.59pm. All of a sudden, and I swear to you I am not making this up, no matter how bizarre it sounds, Pops opened his eyes. He slowly looked to his left, then to his right and then looked straight forward before closing his eyes and letting out his last breath. It was if he was acknowledging all of us before he departed at exactly 2.00pm. It was so strange yet at the same time comforting that we had all been together as a family for the last time and he had somehow managed to say goodbye.

I felt numb as I left the hospital. I knew that he was going to die, and I was glad he was no longer in pain, but all of a sudden I was left without one of the most important people in my life. In a moment of irony, as I reached my car I saw that I had a parking ticket. The ticket was given at exactly 2.00pm, the same time that Pops had passed away. It was a reminder that no matter how much trouble I got myself into, Pops was no longer around to help me out. I was on my own.

In little over a week I had lost my career and my father.

It was a cruel blow and I'm sure many fully expected me to resort to my old ways and start drinking again. To a degree even I thought that after everything that had happened that I would need to start drinking to help numb the pain but I didn't. I thought that it would be doing my father a disservice to use his death as an excuse to ruin my life and everyone else's around me. He had left me in this world sober and I planned to continue that way no matter how much shit was thrown at me. Foremost in my mind was following my father's example, and being a good father to my kids, and drinking most certainly wouldn't have let me do that. I was determined not to let him down. I still wanted him to be proud of me up in heaven and I knew he would be looking down on me keeping me from harm's way.

In those initial months, following the end of my career, and the death of my father, I suffered from unconfined loneliness. I missed the banter of all the boys at Swindon and I felt my father's loss keenly, especially on those Saturday afternoons when we had spent so much time together after my knee operation.

With so much spare time on my hands, and feeling so alone, I needed to find a place that I could hang out to have some company. In the past it would have been the pub, but that was now out of the question, so I stupidly started going to the casino. I had always enjoyed a game of cards and at first I went to the casino to be sociable, sometimes I wouldn't even play, I would merely sit and chat to people. As always, the more you go to a casino you eventually get sucked in and I started playing high stake poker games. Within a few months I had blown at least £20,000, it could have even been much more; I lost count in the end. I squandered most of the money I had received from Swindon at the end of my career and I had nothing to show for it. To make matters worse the people running the sports management company that I had been helping out had been clueless, so I left, but that meant that I now had no money coming in.

I wouldn't say that I had a gambling addiction, I was so consumed with grief and loneliness that I lost track of the sums I was losing. When I realised what I had done I stopped immediately, without the need for rehab, and realised I needed to find somewhere else to go to be sociable.

Unfortunately, whilst my marriage had survived my alcoholism, the premature end of my career and the death of my father, the gambling issues proved too much and Janine and I separated once and for all in September 2009. The relationship had fizzled out and I suppose that, whilst we both still respected each other, we realised that we had fallen out of love.

Julian Keeling, my counsellor at Sporting Chance, once told me that on average only around 5% of marriages survive after one of the couple has successfully completed rehab, therefore the end of our marriage really should have come as no surprise. Janine is a great mother to our two kids and whilst our relationship is over we try our best to raise our children in a loving and stable environment.

With my marriage at an end, I moved out of our home in Pontprennau and moved into Pop's old house in Llanrumney, where I had grown up, as it was now empty. It was strange being back in the house where it had all started, especially without the noise of my brothers and sisters. It felt right to be there and in a way it made me feel close to Pops during a difficult time.

However, after the year from hell, and shortly after my marriage to Janine fell apart, my resolve regarding alcohol snapped. I went up the shops, bought a crate of Stella, took it to my friend's house and was determined to drink every single can. I thought I would have a few days hitting it hard and then would get back to sobriety. Thankfully I didn't crack open a single can and the next day I went straight to AA. It was weird as it felt as if something had overtaken my body and I wasn't in control of myself. When I look back now I can't believe that I even considered drinking alcohol.

In the space of a year I had lost my career, my father, my marriage and almost all my money. It's fair to say that it wasn't the best of times. The only bright spot was the testimonial that Swindon Town granted me.

Despite my issues with Maurice Malpas, Swindon Town Football Club were brilliant. I had only been at the club for four seasons but they offered me a testimonial game, which I gratefully accepted. Typically Gus Poyet, who was assistant manager at Spurs at the time, helped to organise a day that I will never forget.

As Gus was at Spurs, I got in touch and asked if he would be able to get a decent team together for my testimonial. At first he said that it wouldn't be a problem but then he rang me back and said that the manager would only let the reserves play in it. Gus then told me that instead of that he would organise a Chelsea Legends team to play Swindon and that was good enough for me.

Gus invited me to meet him at the Chelsea Hotel, outside Stamford Bridge, in order to discuss the game. Little did I know that it was the same night as the

Chelsea old boys Christmas night out at Marco Pierre White's restaurant. Gus took me with him and I couldn't believe I was in a room with some of the top players in the history of a great club like Chelsea. Dennis Wise was in the room bouncing around, wearing his usual naughty Prada gear, and he introduced me to everyone. As usual Dennis and Gus fussed over me and made me feel special. I swear, whenever I feel low I just need to be in their company and they pick me straight back up.

My testimonial was a sad and great day at the same time. It was sad because it marked the end of my career and my knee was so bad that I couldn't even participate in it. However, Gus managed to persuade the likes of Dennis Wise, Graeme Le Saux, Roberto Di Matteo and Gianfranco Zola to play. I couldn't believe that those guys had turned up to help me and I was grateful to them all. They weren't paid to play, and they didn't know me, but the fact that they turned up because Gus asked them shows the high regard that they all have for him.

Zola was out of this world during the game. I had always been a huge fan of his but watching him close up showed his world-class touch and awareness. I swear, even though he had been retired for a few years, he could still have easily done a job for a professional club. He grabbed a hat trick during the game and I'm sure it was a real treat for the public of Swindon to get a glimpse of a talent like that. As you would expect, Zola was also a top guy and after the game he signed his boots and gave them to me.

The year 2008 hadn't been the best, but when it ended I knew that I had a clean slate to do whatever I wanted to do with my life, and that was invigorating.

17

LOOKING TO
THE FUTURE

I turned 30 on 22 October 2009 and it seemed appropriate to be reaching that milestone as I was set to make a fresh start in life. The first of my 30 years had been an unbelievable roller coaster of unimagined highs and then unmitigated lows. In those 30 years I had already lived a life full of more drama than anyone could expect to have in an entire lifetime.

For instance, I had already seen my dream career come and go, where I had the joy of scoring goals in front of thousands of fans chanting my name, as well as being treated like a pariah by people like Billy Ayre and Maurice Malpas. I had been with my wife since I was 17 years old and she gave me the joy of having children, but we had also lived through the pain of losing two babies, my alcoholism and my gambling problems. During the course of my career I had earned a small fortune and then blown the majority of it on materialistic items, alcohol and gambling, and as George Best famously said, 'the rest I squandered'.

At 30 years of age I was certainly a lot wiser for everything that I had been through. I did really feel that it was a new dawn and that I was back at the beginning; single, jobless and penniless. I wouldn't say that I was too downhearted though; I knew that after everything I had a clean slate and that inspired me.

At times I thought back to the Al Pacino speech that had so motivated me before the play off semi-final against Hartlepool for Bristol City, in particular this part: 'I've made every wrong choice a middle-aged man can make. I pissed away all my money, believe it or not. I chased off anyone who's ever loved me, and lately, I can't even stand the face I see in the mirror'. That pretty much encapsulated what I had done, but the end of the speech always gave me hope: 'We can stay here and get the shit kicked out of us, or we can fight our way back into the light. We can climb out of hell. One inch at a time.'

I truly believed that by taking a small step in the right direction then you are on your way towards redemption. If you keep moving inch by inch you can reach your final goal. My final goal was to become a better person, and over the last few months I really have concentrated on trying to do that 'one inch at a time'.

One of the first steps that I took was towards spiritual enlightenment. I started hanging around at a café in Cardiff called Mazza as I grew fond of smoking the shisha pipes there. One of the big attractions of Mazza was of course the social aspect. I had moved on from the pub, to Starbucks, to the casino and finally to Mazza where I felt at home.

The guys who owned the café were called Obaid, Omaid and Hussein. They made me feel welcome and I spent a lot of time with them. They were from a

Muslim background and as I said previously, the steps that I had taken at AA had left me with an interest in religion as I felt that someone greater than myself had seen me through a difficult time in my life. Indeed, when I left rehab I had tattoos of the Virgin Mary and Jesus inscribed on my arm.

As I spent more time with the guys, I began asking them questions about their religion. A lot of the clientele at Mazza were Muslim and they always seemed peaceful and respectful, and I wanted to experience the same feeling of inner peace that they had. Another attraction was, of course, that you are not allowed to drink alcohol if you are a Muslim.

When I asked about the religion they would tell me about their lives as Muslims. They would never preach, but satisfied my curiosity. I spent a while considering whether to convert, and then on New Year's day I felt I wanted to know even more about the Muslim faith. Obaid offered to take me to the Mosque with him so that I could speak to other people from the religion. Going to the Mosque blew me away and after the experience I was in no doubt that I was ready to convert.

It was not a decision that I took lightly. The Muslim faith has taken a hammering since the events of 9/11, due to a small minority of fanatics distorting what is the true meaning of the *Koran*. I knew that some of my friends and family may not be supportive of my decision, and that was a worry, but since when had I cared what anyone thought of me?

At my conversion ceremony at the Mosque I felt shivers go down my spine, it was an awe-inspiring experience. Even though I still go by the name

'Christian' those at the Mosque call me 'Kareem'. I can honestly say that since I started attending the Mosque I have never encountered so called religious fundamentalists. Every Muslim I have met has been respectful of other faiths and that is important to me. I have always been a tolerant person of people's races and religions and I believe that each religion has something that can speak to each person. Whatever that person needs to do, other than harm others, in order to find peace and happiness in their lives then they should pursue it.

That is one of the reasons I have become so involved in the anti racism campaign since I left football, as it is a subject that is close to my heart. I am, of course, from a mixed parentage background so dealing with racism was important to me. During my time in football, whilst there can be no doubt that racism is not as prevalent as it once was, I did hear racist abuse from time to time directed towards players. As I mentioned earlier in the book, I remember John Williams at Cardiff getting abused when we played Swansea.

I felt that one of the best ways to combat racism was to change the viewpoints of the kids and make them realise that no one deserves to be bullied or abused purely because of the colour of their skin. It does seem crazy in this multicultural age that some people still think less of others because of their skin colour, but as I have seen during my work with the anti racism campaign, the problem still exists.

I spend about three days every week going into schools throughout Wales conducting workshops about anti racism. It's a worthwhile cause which I am happy to dedicate my time to. The kids seem to respect and listen to me purely because I am an ex-professional footballer and if that can help to communicate the anti racism message, then great.

Another project that has given me plenty of joy since I have retired is a football coaching company that I have set up called 'Total Technique'. The primary aim of the company is to get as many girls and boys of all ages and standards playing football together. The company doesn't only focus on the best players; I want all kids from the community to have somewhere to go where they can enjoy themselves. I think it's important in this day and age that kids have an option, other than wondering the streets, where they can have fun and learn all about discipline and team work. Again, my status as an ex-professional seems to carry a lot of weight so kids listen to me. Four local guys Owen, Clem, Umar and Shaq help me out with the coaching and we make a great team—I certainly couldn't do it without them.

I can honestly say that my anti racism work and coaching gives me as much joy as I derived from playing. After taking so much from the game and giving little back when I was drinking, it feels amazing finally to be doing some good. I get a real buzz from changing a kid's attitude towards racism or seeing a youngster learn a new skill and I can see both jobs playing a huge part in my future.

Something else that I have enjoyed since my retirement is doing some media work. I spend time on the Real Radio sports phone in show in South Wales where I talk about the latest football news. I also occasionally commentate on Cardiff City games for BBC Wales. It's great fun working on the shows and it's nice to be amongst fellow ex-professional sportsmen like former Cardiff player David Giles and ex-Welsh rugby international, David Bishop. We always have a great crack and I hope to do a lot more media work in the future.

I always like to have a few projects on the go as I find working in one area bores me. One of the projects that I am about to get off the ground is a charity called 'Live Life Right' which aims to help underprivileged children have a better childhood through sport. This is something that is very close to my heart as I remember struggling to be able to afford the £1.00 entry fee to go swimming when I was a kid and I certainly couldn't afford to go to any summer football schools. With this charity I hope to raise the money, through a number of initiatives, so that children from areas like Llanrumney will be able to have swimming lessons, football coaching or anything else to do with sport that keeps them off the streets and shows them the value of keeping healthy and active.

I am also in the process of setting up my own sports management company called 'Legacy' which I hope will help guide young professional footballers away from the many pitfalls in the game. Having seen the good and the bad side of being a professional footballer, I believe that my experiences will be invaluable when advising young professionals. I have a good staff of lawyers and financial advisors behind me as well and I'm excited to be involved with a sports management company that isn't simply trying to make a quick buck, but is genuinely trying to provide a youngster with the best legal and financial advice so that they can further their career.

After everything that has happened to me, I am blessed that I now have a wonderful new girlfriend, Ceri Prince, who helps keeps me on the straight and narrow. I have known Ceri for years, as she used to be the barmaid at my local pub when I was a teenager. I always used to think she looked hot, but nothing ever happened. Over the years I kept bumping into her, as she lived near Pops, or sometimes I saw her out in town and we would have a chat and talk about old times.

When I moved back to Pops' house, following separating from Janine, I finally joined the Facebook revolution and Ceri and I became friends on there. We started chatting and arranged to meet up for a coffee where she told me about her job as a Department Manager at a local law firm and I filled her in on all the crazy goings on in my life. She still looked fantastic, and after spending some time together, it was obvious we shared a bond so we arranged to meet up again. After a few dates we eventually started a relationship and I am lucky to have met someone as loving as Ceri. We've been together for a few months now, and Ceri has recently met my two boys. I am over the moon about how well they all get on, as that is important to me. Our love for each other grows every day and I believe that we are meant to be together forever. I can't remember the last time I felt so happy.

Ceri has been understanding about my situation, and knows all about my past, so with her alongside me, the absence of drink in my life, and the varied work I am doing, I am finally starting to feel better about myself. I've had more than enough drama over the years and now I'm happy to live a quiet life with someone I love.

After all I've been through I have ended up right where I started, back home in Llanrumney. I don't enjoy all the trappings that my success as a footballer brought me anymore, for instance the flash motors are gone and sometimes I catch the bus, but I can honestly say I'm happier than ever right now. I haven't had a drink since February 2006 but I know that if I want to ruin my life, and everyone else's around me, all I need to do is take one sip of alcohol. In fact I'm convinced that one sip would lead to me killing myself because after so long without touching the stuff I would drown myself in an ocean of it. I always say to people that I live my life with a loaded gun and if I want to kill myself I don't need a bullet, I just need a can of Stella.

Whilst I have been sober for over four years now, I try not to plan too far ahead, or think too much about my issues, as otherwise I will drive myself crazy. If I can get through each day sober then that is another victory for me. Tomorrow could be the day when I finally crack and have a drink but I take each day at a time and I find that this approach has helped me to remain sober so far.

As I was coming towards the end of this book I saw a quote by the former Chelsea manager, Jose Mourinho, which seemed to sum up my life perfectly. He said: 'There's a history made up by each of us, that leads us to that final victory, it's that history, in its entirety, that turns us into champions.'

I feel that Mourinho is saying that a person's entire past, both good and bad, can turn that individual into a champion if they have learnt from their previous mistakes. I've done plenty of bad things in my life, which I am ashamed of, but over time I believe that I have learnt from those mistakes and that has turned me into the happy person that I am today, where I try my best to put the well being of others before myself. If I hadn't had made those mistakes I would not be the person that I am today. I'm by no means perfect, I'm still a work in progress and in the future I may slip, but every day I'm learning to become a better person. At the end of my life I hope that my kids will say the sort of things about me that I say about my own father. If they do then I know my mission will have been accomplished.

Who knows how my life will pan out? As long as I'm happy, and those I love are happy as well, then I can't ask for more.

I hope you've enjoyed hearing about my life. It's not all glamour being a footballer, but after all my ups and downs it has certainly provided me with a story to tell. The most important thing for me is that this book might encourage someone to seek help for their own addiction issues. If it does then everything I have been through will have been worth it.

APPENDIX

Games played by Christian Roberts in 1997/1998   **Goals**   **Cards**

		Goals	Cards
13–09–1997	Football League Two - **Cardiff** 2–1 Rochdale	0	
08–03–1998	Football League Two - Swansea 1–1 **Cardiff**	0	
14–03–1998	Football League Two - **Cardiff** 7–1 Doncaster	1	
21–03–1998	Football League Two - Hull 0–1 **Cardiff**	1	
28–03–1998	Football League Two - **Cardiff** 0–0 Brighton	0	
03–04–1998	Football League Two - Scarborough 3–1 **Cardiff**	0	
11–04–1998	Football League Two - **Cardiff** 0–2 Colchester	0	
13–04–1998	Football League Two - Peterborough 2–0 **Cardiff**	0	
18–04–1998	Football League Two - **Cardiff** 1–2 Macclesfield	1	
25–04–1998	Football League Two - Hartlepool 2–0 **Cardiff**	0	
02–05–1998	Football League Two - **Cardiff** 0–0 Darlington	0	

Goals: 3   **Yellow cards: 0**   **Red Cards: 0**

Games played by Christian Roberts in 1998/1999   **Goals**   **Cards**

		Goals	Cards
11–08–1998	English League Cup - Fulham 2–1 **Cardiff**	0	
18–08–1998	English League Cup - **Cardiff** 1–2 Fulham	0	
31–10–1998	Football League Two - **Cardiff** 1–0 Exeter	0	
07–11–1998	Football League Two - Torquay 0–0 **Cardiff**	0	
14–11–1998	English FA Cup - **Cardiff** 6–0 Chester	0	
28–11–1998	Football League Two - **Cardiff** 2–0 Southend	0	
09–12–1998	Football League Trophy - Millwall 2–0 **Cardiff**	0	
02–01–1999	English FA Cup - **Cardiff** 1–1 Yeovil	0	
08–05–1999	Football League Two - Mansfield 3–0 **Cardiff**	0	

Goals: 0   **Yellow cards: 1**   **Red Cards: 0**

Games played by Christian Roberts in 1999/2000   **Goals**   **Cards**

		Goals	Cards
11–09–1999	Football League One - Wycombe 3–1 **Cardiff**	0	
02–11–1999	Football League One - **Cardiff** 1–1 Blackpool	0	
09–11–1999	English FA Cup - **Cardiff** 3–1 Leyton Orient	0	
12–11–1999	Football League One - **Cardiff** 2–1 Chesterfield	0	
20–11–1999	English FA Cup - Bury 0–0 **Cardiff**	0	
23–11–1999	Football League One - Colchester 0–3 **Cardiff**	0	
27–11–1999	Football League One - **Cardiff** 1–2 Gillingham	0	Y
30–11–1999	English FA Cup - **Cardiff** 1–0 Bury	0	
04–12–1999	Football League One - Millwall 2–0 **Cardiff**	0	
07–12–1999	Football League Trophy - Northampton 1–0 **Cardiff**	0	
09–01–2000	Football League One - Bristol C 0–0 **Cardiff**	0	
21–03–2000	Football League One - Chesterfield 1–1 **Cardiff**	0	

Goals: 0   **Yellow cards: 1**   **Red Cards: 0**

Games played by Christian Roberts in 2000/2001

		Goals	Cards
12–08–2000	Football League Two - **Exeter** 1–2 Cardiff	0	Y
19–08–2000	Football League Two - Darlington 1–1 **Exeter**	0	
22–08–2000	English League Cup - Swindon 1–1 **Exeter**	0	
26–08–2000	Football League Two - **Exeter** 1–1 Hartlepool	1	
28–08–2000	Football League Two - Leyton Orient 2–1 **Exeter**	0	
02–09–2000	Football League Two - **Exeter** 0–0 Mansfield	0	
05–09–2000	English League Cup - **Exeter** 1–2 Swindon	0	
09–09–2000	Football League Two - Macclesfield 0–2 **Exeter**	1	
12–09–2000	Football League Two - Barnet 1–1 **Exeter**	0	
16–09–2000	Football League Two - **Exeter** 3–1 York	2	
23–09–2000	Football League Two - Carlisle 0–1 **Exeter**	0	Y
30–09–2000	Football League Two - **Exeter** 0–2 Cheltenham	0	
06–10–2000	Football League Two - Shrewsbury 2–0 **Exeter**	0	
14–10–2000	Football League Two - **Exeter** 1–1 Chesterfield	0	
17–10–2000	Football League Two - **Exeter** 0–1 Hull	0	
21–10–2000	Football League Two - Kidderminster 0–0 **Exeter**	0	
24–10–2000	Football League Two - Southend 1–1 **Exeter**	0	Y
28–10–2000	Football League Two - **Exeter** 0–1 Rochdale	0	
04–11–2000	Football League Two - Halifax 3–1 **Exeter**	0	
11–11–2000	Football League Two - **Exeter** 2–1 Scunthorpe	0	
18–11–2000	English FA Cup - Walsall 4–0 **Exeter**	0	
25–11–2000	Football League Two - Lincoln 3–1 **Exeter**	0	Y
02–12–2000	Football League Two - **Exeter** 0–2 Plymouth	0	
05–12–2000	Football League Trophy - Wycombe 1–0 **Exeter**	0	
09–12–2000	Football League Two - Chesterfield 2–0 **Exeter**	0	Y
16–12–2000	Football League Two - Blackpool 3–0 **Exeter**	0	
13–01–2001	Football League Two - **Exeter** 2–3 Leyton Orient	0	
20–01–2001	Football League Two - Torquay 2–1 **Exeter**	0	
27–01–2001	Football League Two - **Exeter** 1–0 Brighton	0	
02–02–2001	Football League Two - Mansfield 1–1 **Exeter**	0	Y
10–02–2001	Football League Two - **Exeter** 0–0 Macclesfield	0	
17–02–2001	Football League Two - York 0–3 **Exeter**	1	
20–02–2001	Football League Two - **Exeter** 1–0 Barnet	0	
24–02–2001	Football League Two - **Exeter** 1–0 Carlisle	1	
03–03–2001	Football League Two - Cheltenham 1–0 **Exeter**	0	
10–03–2001	Football League Two - **Exeter** 1–0 Shrewsbury	0	
17–03–2001	Football League Two - Hull 2–1 **Exeter**	0	
24–03–2001	Football League Two - **Exeter** 2–1 Kidderminster	0	
27–03–2001	Football League Two - **Exeter** 1–1 Darlington	0	Y
31–03–2001	Football League Two - **Exeter** 2–0 Blackpool	0	
07–04–2001	Football League Two - Plymouth 1–0 **Exeter**	0	Y
14–04–2001	Football League Two - **Exeter** 2–2 Southend	0	
16–04–2001	Football League Two - Rochdale 3–0 **Exeter**	0	
21–04–2001	Football League Two - **Exeter** 0–0 Halifax	0	
28–04–2001	Football League Two - Scunthorpe 0–2 **Exeter**	1	Y
05–05–2001	Football League Two - **Exeter** 0–0 Lincoln	0	

Goals: 7   Yellow cards: 9   Red Cards: 0

Games played by Christian Roberts in 2001/2002		Goals	Cards
11–08–2001	Football League Two - **Exeter** 1–3 Hull	0	
18–08–2001	Football League Two - Halifax 1–1 **Exeter**	0	
21–08–2001	English League Cup - **Exeter** 0–1 Walsall	0	Y
25–08–2001	Football League Two - **Exeter** 0–4 Scunthorpe	0	Y
27–08–2001	Football League Two - Rochdale 2–0 **Exeter**	0	
01–09–2001	Football League Two - **Exeter** 2–2 Luton	0	
08–09–2001	Football League Two - Swansea 4–2 **Exeter**	1	
15–09–2001	Football League Two - **Exeter** 3–2 Oxford	0	
18–09–2001	Football League Two - **Exeter** 2–3 Plymouth	1	
22–09–2001	Football League Two - Darlington 4–0 **Exeter**	0	
25–09–2001	Football League Two - **Exeter** 1–1 Rushden	0	R
29–09–2001	Football League Two - **Exeter** 0–0 Macclesfield	0	Y
06–10–2001	Football League Two - York 2–3 **Exeter**	2	
16–10–2001	Football League Trophy - **Exeter** 1–2 Cambridge U	0	
20–10–2001	Football League Two - Cheltenham 3–1 **Exeter**	1	
23–10–2001	Football League Two - **Exeter** 1–0 Bristol R	0	
27–10–2001	Football League Two - Lincoln 0–0 **Exeter**	0	Y
03–11–2001	Football League Two - **Exeter** 2–1 Southend	1	
10–11–2001	Football League Two - Hartlepool 2–0 **Exeter**	0	
24–11–2001	Football League Two - **Exeter** 0–0 Leyton Orient	0	
01–12–2001	Football League Two - Shrewsbury 0–1 **Exeter**	0	Y
08–12–2001	English FA Cup - **Exeter** 0–0 Dag & Red	0	
19–12–2001	English FA Cup - Dag & Red 3–0 **Exeter**	0	Y
21–12–2001	Football League Two - Mansfield 0–1 **Exeter**	0	
26–12–2001	Football League Two - **Exeter** 0–3 Swansea	0	
29–12–2001	Football League Two - **Exeter** 1–1 Rochdale	0	Y
12–01–2002	Football League Two - **Exeter** 0–0 Halifax	0	
15–01–2002	Football League Two - Scunthorpe 3–4 **Exeter**	2	Y
19–01–2002	Football League Two - Hull 2–0 **Exeter**	0	
22–01–2002	Football League Two - **Exeter** 0–1 Mansfield	0	
02–02–2002	Football League Two - Macclesfield 1–2 **Exeter**	0	
09–02–2002	Football League Two - **Exeter** 0–2 Cheltenham	0	Y
16–02–2002	Football League Two - Carlisle 1–0 **Exeter**	0	
23–02–2002	Football League Two - Oxford 1–2 **Exeter**	0	
26–02–2002	Football League Two - Plymouth 3–0 **Exeter**	0	
02–03–2002	Football League Two - **Exeter** 4–2 Darlington	2	
05–03–2002	Football League Two - Rushden 2–1 **Exeter**	0	
09–03–2002	Football League Two - Kidderminster 3–1 **Exeter**	0	Y
12–03–2002	Football League Two - Luton 3–0 **Exeter**	0	
16–03–2002	Football League Two - **Exeter** 2–2 Shrewsbury	0	
19–03–2002	Football League Two - **Exeter** 2–1 York	1	Y
01–04–2002	Football League One - Brighton 2–1 **Bristol C**	0	
06–04–2002	Football League One - **Bristol C** 2–0 Bury	0	
13–04–2002	Football League One - Blackpool 5–1 **Bristol C**	0	Y
20–04–2002	Football League One - **Bristol C** 1–1 Stoke	0	

Goals: 11   Yellow cards: 12   Red Cards: 1

Games played by Christian Roberts in 2002/2003

Date	Match	Goals	Cards
10–08–2002	Football League One - **Bristol C** 2–0 Blackpool	0	
13–08–2002	Football League One - Brentford 1–0 **Bristol C**	0	
17–08–2002	Football League One - Wigan 2–0 **Bristol C**	0	
24–08–2002	Football League One - **Bristol C** 3–0 Wycombe	1	Y
26–08–2002	Football League One - Plymouth 2–0 **Bristol C**	0	
31–08–2002	Football League One - **Bristol C** 2–0 Tranmere	0	
06–09–2002	Football League One - **Bristol C** 3–0 Northampton	0	
10–09–2002	English League Cup - **Bristol C** 0–1 Oxford	0	
14–09–2002	Football League One - Cheltenham 2–3 **Bristol C**	0	
17–09–2002	Football League One - Oldham 1–0 **Bristol C**	0	
21–09–2002	Football League One - **Bristol C** 1–3 QPR	0	
28–09–2002	Football League One - Port Vale 2–3 **Bristol C**	0	
05–10–2002	Football League One - **Bristol C** 4–0 Chesterfield	1	
12–10–2002	Football League One - Barnsley 1–4 **Bristol C**	3	
19–10–2002	Football League One - **Bristol C** 2–0 Swindon	0	
22–10–2002	Football League Trophy - QPR 0–0 **Bristol C**	0	Y
26–10–2002	Football League One - Peterborough 1–3 **Bristol C**	0	
29–10–2002	Football League One - **Bristol C** 1–0 Huddersfield	0	
09–11–2002	Football League One - Colchester 2–2 **Bristol C**	0	Y
13–11–2002	Football League Trophy - Boston Utd 1–2 **Bristol C**	0	
16–11–2002	English FA Cup - Heybridge 0–7 **Bristol C**	2	
23–11–2002	Football League One - Mansfield 4–5 **Bristol C**	2	
30–11–2002	Football League One - **Bristol C** 2–2 Crewe	0	
03–12–2002	Football League One - **Bristol C** 3–2 Notts Co	0	
08–12–2002	English FA Cup - Harrogate Railway 1–3 **Bristol C**	1	
14–12–2002	Football League One - Cardiff 0–2 **Bristol C**	1	
21–12–2002	Football League One - **Bristol C** 1–1 Luton	0	Y
26–12–2002	Football League One - **Bristol C** 0–0 Plymouth	0	Y
01–01–2003	Football League One - Wycombe 2–1 **Bristol C**	0	
04–01–2003	English FA Cup - Leicester 2–0 **Bristol C**	0	
18–01–2003	Football League One - Tranmere 1–1 **Bristol C**	0	Y
21–01–2003	Football League Trophy - Bournemouth 1–3 **Bristol C**	0	
25–01–2003	Football League One - **Bristol C** 1–1 Stockport	1	
01–02–2003	Football League One - Blackpool 0–0 **Bristol C**	0	
08–02–2003	Football League One - **Bristol C** 1–2 Colchester	0	
11–02–2003	Football League One - **Bristol C** 0–0 Brentford	0	
15–02–2003	Football League One - Notts Co 2–0 **Bristol C**	0	
18–02–2003	Football League Trophy - **Bristol C** 4–2 Cambridge U	0	
22–02–2003	Football League One - Northampton 1–2 **Bristol C**	0	
25–02–2003	Football League Trophy - Cambridge U 0–3 **Bristol C**	1	
01–03–2003	Football League One - **Bristol C** 3–1 Cheltenham	0	
04–03–2003	Football League One - **Bristol C** 2–0 Oldham	1	
08–03–2003	Football League One - QPR 1–0 **Bristol C**	0	
15–03–2003	Football League One - **Bristol C** 1–0 Peterborough	0	
19–03–2003	Football League One - Swindon 1–1 **Bristol C**	0	
22–03–2003	Football League One - Huddersfield 1–2 **Bristol C**	0	

Games played by Christian Roberts in 2002/2003		Goals	Cards
29–03–2003	Football League One - **Bristol C** 2–0 Barnsley	1	
06–04–2003	Football League Trophy - **Bristol C** 2–0 Carlisle	0	
12–04–2003	Football League One - **Bristol C** 5–2 Mansfield	0	
15–04–2003	Football League One - Crewe 1–1 **Bristol C**	1	
19–04–2003	Football League One - Luton 2–2 **Bristol C**	0	
22–04–2003	Football League One - **Bristol C** 2–0 Cardiff	1	
26–04–2003	Football League One - Chesterfield 2–0 **Bristol C**	0	
03–05–2003	Football League One - **Bristol C** 2–0 Port Vale	0	
10–05–2003	League One Play-Off - Cardiff 1–0 **Bristol C**	0	Y
13–05–2003	League One Play-Off - **Bristol C** 0–0 Cardiff	0	

Goals: 17   Yellow cards: 7   Red Cards: 0

Games played by Christian Roberts in 2003/2004		Goals	Cards
09–08–2003	Football League One - **Bristol C** 5–0 Notts Co	0	
13–08–2003	English League Cup - **Bristol C** 4–1 Swansea	0	
16–08–2003	Football League One - Chesterfield 1–1 **Bristol C**	0	
23–08–2003	Football League One - **Bristol C** 1–1 Hartlepool	0	
26–08–2003	Football League One - Colchester 2–1 **Bristol C**	0	Y
30–08–2003	Football League One - **Bristol C** 1–0 Grimsby	1	
06–09–2003	Football League One - Bournemouth 0–0 **Bristol C**	0	
13–09–2003	Football League One - Oldham 1–1 **Bristol C**	0	
16–09–2003	Football League One - **Bristol C** 2–0 Tranmere	0	Y
20–09–2003	Football League One - **Bristol C** 0–1 Port Vale	0	
23–09–2003	English League Cup - **Bristol C** 1–0 Watford	0	
27–09–2003	Football League One - QPR 1–1 **Bristol C**	0	
04–10–2003	Football League One - **Bristol C** 2–1 Swindon	0	
10–10–2003	Football League One - **Bristol C** 1–1 Peterborough	0	
14–10–2003	Football League Trophy - Plymouth 4–0 **Bristol C**	0	
18–10–2003	Football League One - Wrexham 0–0 **Bristol C**	0	Y
21–10–2003	Football League One - Wycombe 3–0 **Bristol C**	0	
25–10–2003	Football League One - **Bristol C** 1–1 Sheff Wed	0	
28–10–2003	English League Cup - **Bristol C** 0–3 Southampton	0	
01–11–2003	Football League One - **Bristol C** 1–1 Luton	0	
09–11–2003	English FA Cup - Bradford PA 2–5 **Bristol C**	0	
15–11–2003	Football League One - Brighton 1–4 **Bristol C**	0	
22–11–2003	Football League One - **Bristol C** 2–1 Barnsley	0	
29–11–2003	Football League One - Blackpool 1–0 **Bristol C**	0	
06–12–2003	English FA Cup - **Bristol C** 0–0 Barnsley	0	
13–12–2003	Football League One - Rushden 1–1 **Bristol C**	0	
16–12–2003	English FA Cup - Barnsley 2–1 **Bristol C**	1	Y
20–12–2003	Football League One - **Bristol C** 1–0 Stockport	0	Y
26–12–2003	Football League One - Brentford 1–2 **Bristol C**	0	
28–12–2003	Football League One - **Bristol C** 2–0 Bournemouth	0	
27–01–2004	Football League One - **Bristol C** 1–0 Colchester	0	
07–02–2004	Football League One - **Bristol C** 3–1 Brentford	0	
28–02–2004	Football League One - Sheff Wed 1–0 **Bristol C**	0	

Games played by Christian Roberts in 2003/2004	Goals	Cards

Date	Match	Goals	Cards
06–03–2004	Football League One - Stockport 2–0 **Bristol C**	0	
12–03–2004	Football League One - **Bristol C** 1–0 Rushden	0	
20–03–2004	Football League One - **Bristol C** 0–2 Oldham	0	
24–03–2004	Football League One - Tranmere 1–0 **Bristol C**	0	
27–03–2004	Football League One - Port Vale 2–1 **Bristol C**	0	
03–04–2004	Football League One - **Bristol C** 1–0 QPR	1	
10–04–2004	Football League One - Swindon 1–1 **Bristol C**	1	Y
13–04–2004	Football League One - **Bristol C** 1–0 Plymouth	0	Y
17–04–2004	Football League One - Luton 3–2 **Bristol C**	1	
24–04–2004	Football League One - **Bristol C** 0–0 Brighton	0	
02–05–2004	Football League One - Barnsley 0–1 **Bristol C**	0	
08–05–2004	Football League One - **Bristol C** 2–1 Blackpool	2	Y
15–05–2004	League One Play-Off - Hartlepool 1–1 **Bristol C**	0	
19–05–2004	League One Play-Off - **Bristol C** 2–1 Hartlepool	1	Y
30–05–2004	League One Play-Off - **Bristol C** 0–1 Brighton	0	

Goals: 8   Yellow cards: 10   Red Cards: 0

Games played by Christian Roberts in 2004/2005	Goals	Cards

Date	Match	Goals	Cards
07–08–2004	Football League One - **Bristol C** 1–1 Torquay	0	
21–08–2004	Football League One - **Bristol C** 1–2 Swindon	0	Y
24–08–2004	English League Cup - Wycombe 0–1 **Bristol C**	0	Y
28–08–2004	Football League One - Port Vale 3–0 **Bristol C**	0	
30–08–2004	Football League One - **Bristol C** 4–1 Brentford	0	
04–09–2004	Football League One - Peterborough 0–1 **Bristol C**	0	
11–09–2004	Football League One - **Bristol C** 5–0 Stockport	1	
18–09–2004	Football League One - Bradford 4–1 **Bristol C**	0	
22–09–2004	English League Cup - **Bristol C** 2–2 Everton	0	
25–09–2004	Football League One - **Bristol C** 3–3 Huddersfield	0	
16–10–2004	Football League One - **Swindon** 1–0 Oldham	1	
19–10–2004	Football League One - Port Vale 1–0 **Swindon**	0	
23–10–2004	Football League One - Barnsley 2–2 **Swindon**	1	Y
27–10–2004	Football League One - **Swindon** 3–2 Sheff Wed	0	
30–10–2004	Football League One - **Swindon** 3–3 Torquay	0	
06–11–2004	Football League One - Tranmere 2–1 **Swindon**	0	
13–11–2004	English FA Cup - **Swindon** 4–1 Sheff Wed	1	
20–11–2004	Football League One - **Swindon** 4–2 Hull	1	
27–11–2004	Football League One - Chesterfield 1–0 **Swindon**	0	Y
08–12–2004	Football League One - **Swindon** 1–2 Huddersfield	0	
11–12–2004	Football League One - **Swindon** 1–1 Doncaster	0	
15–12–2004	English FA Cup - Notts Co 2–0 **Swindon**	0	
18–12–2004	Football League One - Bournemouth 2–1 **Swindon**	0	Y
26–12–2004	Football League One - Peterborough 0–2 **Swindon**	0	
12–03–2005	Football League One - Luton 3–1 **Swindon**	0	
19–03–2005	Football League One - **Swindon** 4–2 Wrexham	0	
25–03–2005	Football League One - MK Dons 1–1 **Swindon**	0	
02–04–2005	Football League One - Hartlepool 3–0 **Swindon**	0	

Games played by Christian Roberts in 2004/2005	Goals	Cards
09–04–2005 Football League One - **Swindon** 1–2 Walsall	0	
16–04–2005 Football League One - Hull 0–0 **Swindon**	0	
23–04–2005 Football League One - **Swindon** 2–1 Tranmere	0	
30–04–2005 Football League One - Huddersfield 4–0 **Swindon**	0	
07–05–2005 Football League One - **Swindon** 1–1 Chesterfield	0	

Goals: 5   Yellow cards: 5   Red Cards: 0

Games played by Christian Roberts in 2005/2006	Goals	Cards
06–08–2005 Football League One - Barnsley 2–0 **Swindon**	0	Y
09–08–2005 Football League One - **Swindon** 2–3 Oldham	1	
13–08–2005 Football League One - **Swindon** 2–1 Nottm Forest	0	
20–08–2005 Football League One - Blackpool 0–0 **Swindon**	0	
23–08–2005 English League Cup - **Swindon** 1–3 Wycombe	0	
27–08–2005 Football League One - **Swindon** 4–2 Yeovil	1	
29–08–2005 Football League One - Tranmere 1–0 **Swindon**	0	
03–09–2005 Football League One - Walsall 1–0 **Swindon**	0	
10–09–2005 Football League One - **Swindon** 1–2 Southend	0	
17–09–2005 Football League One - Bournemouth 2–1 **Swindon**	0	
24–09–2005 Football League One - **Swindon** 2–3 Bradford	0	
27–09–2005 Football League One - Doncaster 1–0 **Swindon**	0	
15–10–2005 Football League One - Brentford 0–0 **Swindon**	0	
18–10–2005 Football League Trophy - **Swindon** 2–0 Stevenage	0	
22–10–2005 Football League One - **Swindon** 1–1 Scunthorpe	1	
11–11–2005 Football League One - **Swindon** 2–1 Bristol C	0	
16–11–2005 English FA Cup - Boston Utd 4–1 **Swindon**	0	Y
19–11–2005 Football League One - Port Vale 1–1 **Swindon**	0	
22–11–2005 Football League Trophy - Peterborough 2–1 **Swindon**	1	
26–11–2005 Football League One - **Swindon** 0–3 Barnsley	0	Y
03–12–2005 Football League One - Rotherham 0–1 **Swindon**	0	
11–02–2006 Football League One - Bradford 1–1 **Swindon**	0	
18–02–2006 Football League One - **Swindon** 2–3 Rotherham	0	
18–03–2006 Football League One - Colchester 1–0 **Swindon**	0	

Goals: 4   Yellow cards: 3   Red Cards: 0

Games played by Christian Roberts in 2006/2007	Goals	Cards
05–08–2006 Football League Two - Hartlepool 0–1 **Swindon**	0	Y
08–08–2006 Football League Two - **Swindon** 2–1 Barnet	0	
12–08–2006 Football League Two - **Swindon** 1–0 Rochdale	0	
19–08–2006 Football League Two - Darlington 1–2 **Swindon**	1	
26–08–2006 Football League Two - **Swindon** 2–0 Stockport	1	
01–09–2006 Football League Two - Chester 0–2 **Swindon**	0	
09–09–2006 Football League Two - Wrexham 2–1 **Swindon**	0	
12–09–2006 Football League Two - **Swindon** 2–1 MK Dons	0	Y
16–09–2006 Football League Two - **Swindon** 0–1 Peterborough	0	
23–09–2006 Football League Two - Notts Co 1–1 **Swindon**	0	Y
26–09–2006 Football League Two - Wycombe 1–1 **Swindon**	0	

Games played by Christian Roberts in 2006/2007   **Goals**   **Cards**

Date	Match	Goals	Cards
30–09–2006	Football League Two - **Swindon** 1–1 Boston Utd	0	
07–10–2006	Football League Two - Accrington 1–1 **Swindon**	0	
04–11–2006	Football League Two - **Swindon** 1–2 Hereford	1	
11–11–2006	English FA Cup - **Swindon** 3–1 Carlisle	2	
18–11–2006	Football League Two - Torquay 0–1 **Swindon**	1	
25–11–2006	Football League Two - **Swindon** 2–1 Bury	1	
02–12–2006	English FA Cup - **Swindon** 1–0 Morecambe	1	Y
05–12–2006	Football League Two - Mansfield 2–0 **Swindon**	0	
09–12–2006	Football League Two - Walsall 0–2 **Swindon**	1	
16–12–2006	Football League Two - **Swindon** 2–1 Bristol R	0	Y
26–12–2006	Football League Two - **Swindon** 2–1 Wycombe	0	
30–12–2006	Football League Two - **Swindon** 1–1 Notts Co	0	
01–01–2007	Football League Two - MK Dons 0–1 **Swindon**	0	
06–01–2007	English FA Cup - C Palace 2–1 **Swindon**	0	
13–01–2007	Football League Two - **Swindon** 2–1 Wrexham	1	
20–01–2007	Football League Two - Boston Utd 1–3 **Swindon**	1	
27–01–2007	Football League Two - **Swindon** 2–0 Macclesfield	0	Y
30–01–2007	Football League Two - Peterborough 1–1 **Swindon**	0	
03–02–2007	Football League Two - **Swindon** 0–1 Hartlepool	0	
17–02–2007	Football League Two - **Swindon** 1–1 Darlington	0	
20–02–2007	Football League Two - Barnet 1–0 **Swindon**	0	Y
24–02–2007	Football League Two - **Swindon** 1–0 Chester	0	
03–03–2007	Football League Two - Stockport 3–0 **Swindon**	0	
10–03–2007	Football League Two - **Swindon** 2–0 Accrington	0	
17–03–2007	Football League Two - Grimsby 1–0 **Swindon**	0	
25–03–2007	Football League Two - Lincoln 2–3 **Swindon**	1	
31–03–2007	Football League Two - **Swindon** 2–1 Shrewsbury	1	
03–04–2007	Football League Two - Rochdale 0–0 **Swindon**	0	
07–04–2007	Football League Two - Hereford 0–0 **Swindon**	0	Y
09–04–2007	Football League Two - **Swindon** 2–1 Torquay	0	
14–04–2007	Football League Two - Bury 0–1 **Swindon**	0	
21–04–2007	Football League Two - **Swindon** 2–0 Mansfield	0	
28–04–2007	Football League Two - Bristol R 1–0 **Swindon**	0	
05–05–2007	Football League Two - **Swindon** 1–1 Walsall	0	Y

Goals: 13   **Yellow cards: 9**   **Red Cards: 0**

Games played by Christian Roberts in 2007/2008   **Goals**   **Cards**

Date	Match	Goals	Cards
11–08–2007	Football League One - Northampton 1–1 **Swindon**	1	
14–08–2007	English League Cup - **Swindon** 0–2 Charlton	0	
18–08–2007	Football League One - **Swindon** 2–1 Luton	0	
25–08–2007	Football League One - Cheltenham 1–1 **Swindon**	0	Y
01–09–2007	Football League One - **Swindon** 1–1 Crewe	0	
09–09–2007	Football League One - **Swindon** 0–1 Yeovil	0	
15–09–2007	Football League One - Hartlepool 1–1 **Swindon**	0	
22–09–2007	Football League One - **Swindon** 4–1 Bournemouth	0	
29–09–2007	Football League One - Millwall 1–2 **Swindon**	0	

Games played by Christian Roberts in 2007/2008		Goals	Cards
02–10–2007	Football League One - Swansea 2–1 **Swindon**	1	Y
06–10–2007	Football League One - **Swindon** 5–0 Gillingham	0	
09–10–2007	Football League Trophy - **Swindon** 1–3 Cheltenham	0	
20–10–2007	Football League One - **Swindon** 1–0 Tranmere	0	
27–10–2007	Football League One - Port Vale 2–1 **Swindon**	0	
03–11–2007	Football League One - **Swindon** 1–2 Doncaster	0	
06–11–2007	Football League One - **Swindon** 1–1 Leyton Orient	0	
10–11–2007	English FA Cup - Wycombe 1–2 **Swindon**	1	
17–11–2007	Football League One - Leeds 2–1 **Swindon**	0	Y
24–11–2007	Football League One - **Swindon** 1–0 Bristol R	1	
01–12–2007	English FA Cup - **Swindon** 3–2 Forest Green	0	
05–01–2008	English FA Cup - **Swindon** 1–1 Barnet	0	
12–01–2008	Football League One - Walsall 2–2 **Swindon**	0	
22–01–2008	English FA Cup - Barnet 1–1 **Swindon**	0	
26–01–2008	Football League One - Crewe 0–0 **Swindon**	0	
29–01–2008	Football League One - Luton 0–1 **Swindon**	1	
02–02–2008	Football League One - **Swindon** 1–1 Northampton	0	
09–02–2008	Football League One - Huddersfield 1–0 **Swindon**	0	
12–02–2008	Football League One - **Swindon** 3–0 Cheltenham	1	
16–02–2008	Football League One - Nottm Forest 1–0 **Swindon**	0	
23–02–2008	Football League One - **Swindon** 0–3 Walsall	0	
26–02–2008	Football League One - Oldham 2–2 **Swindon**	0	
01–03–2008	Football League One - **Swindon** 0–1 Leeds	0	
04–03–2008	Football League One - **Swindon** 3–2 Huddersfield	0	

Goals: 6   Yellow cards: 3   Red Cards: 0